Soon the Antichrist Shall be Revealed

The real history of the man who beat the Universal Church in Court

Grigore Avram Valeriu

Copyright © 2016

Alpha Academic Press

Published in the United States of America

COPYRIGHT DISCLAIMER

Soon the Antichrist Shall be Revealed

First Edition, **Paperback**

Published **November 2016**

Alpha Academic Press

ISBN: **978-0-9975603-2-9**

ABSTRACT

Slush fund, charlatanism and witch doctoring. What church would adopt such methods? A judgment given by the courts of the State of Rio de Janeiro in 1995 proves that there is evidence of such practices in the Universal Church and condemns this religious institution to return the property to the lawyer and college professor Grigore Avram Valeriu.

In this book, Grigore Valeriu gives an account of his entire life, from birth in Romania as a descendant of a traditional Jewish family that came to Brazil when he was 17 years old, until his graduation from Law School and building a solid **patrimony**, lost to the Universal Church. In 1988, undermined by marital and family problems, he looked for help from the church. The aid he received, however, was, besides the loss of his patrimony, the near destruction of his marriage and family.

For the church, the lawyer lost homes, apartments, shops and assets from the stock market. With dilapidated assets and without an alternative, Grigore accepted the invitation of the Universal Church to work as a lawyer. Three months later, this Romanian national took charge of their legal department in Rio de Janeiro. Soon he headed up the national legal department of the Universal Church, in São Paulo, during the period following the purchase of Record Television. He watched closely as illegal practices transpired, suggestions for buying a judge and sermons that did not fit with the conduct of Bishops and pastors. In disagreeing with the actions taken by the church, Grigore was fired. He decided to take legal action to recover his lost property.

This publication originally released in Brazil and propagation in English to help millions of faithful, deceived by sermons based on financial sacrifice to achieve blessings from God, to get rid of these lies and follow, only and exclusively to God, thus being an autobiography that could shake the structures of the religious establishment.

PROLOGUE

A biblical civil suit is the junction where laws and faith come together. A kind of David and Goliath, but as if a Hollywood writer added new elements in order to make the story more interesting.

Actually, David and Goliath were very close before the incident. David had the chance of being Goliath's savior, considered as a savior of humanity. Later on, when the monster showed his true colors, David had to fight him, although he knew Goliath's weaknesses.

The characters now have a new role. David, although smaller than the giant, was a brilliant lawyer with no cases lost. However, the shadows of the past kept following him. He was born in Romania under Nazism when Hitler had already succumbed. In his place, Communism was far from bringing redemption. On the contrary, his childhood was lived in a police state. This Jewish family lived under the masks in the Nazism years: when David was born, his family had to create a last name, which would hide their origins. The rich family became poor during the reign of the Red Army.

David grew up in this type of environment, which remained with him for the rest of his life. He went from wealth to poverty many times. He had twelve realties, but hungered. Having a sick mother, he didn't have any affectionate relationships until he was 30. He ran away from his country to a so-called lost paradise: Brazil. David abnegated Judaism, then God, and finally became a zealous Christian.

That is when he met Goliath. From the top of the pulpit, the giant promised David all that life took from him. Peace, happiness and wealth were within his reach. He only had to surrender himself, body and soul.

Surrender, however, has a price. In this case, it was money itself. David gave all he had: jewelry, apartments, cars and the harmony in his marriage. David saw Goliath committing terrible crimes. Another misunderstood man being destroyed, not so common in history. For Goliath, David would sacrifice even his own life.

In the meantime, he fought the Devil himself, which insisted on whispering in his ear that Goliath was a cheater. Doubt was at his door. Until the day that David found out that it was not the Devil but God who whispered the truth about Goliath.

There was no other way but to face the monster. He did and he failed. Once again, David fell, Goliath won.

After nine months of prayer, David decided to go back to the battlefield, now it was a courtroom. With the bible in one hand and the civil code in the other, David – a lawyer himself – would try to prove that Goliath was the fake prophet that manipulated the souls of his flock. On the other hand, the best lawyers hired by Goliath would protect him attacking not the facts but the man: David was a lunatic liar.

His life would be the focus. All he lived up to now was the subject of the proceedings. David would have to explain himself with lucidity and truth. His personal life of purgatory and hell arose in a decisive moment, in which the verdict could be his eternal conviction or the paradise he was looking for.

The proceedings for David did not only deal with earthly matters. It was about the spirit. To the jurists cited by Goliath's lawyers, David answered with Peter's prophecies. To the cold laws and decrees, the heat of the Apocalypse.

It was without a doubt a proceeding like no other. On one-side was Grigore Valeriu, the lawyer, in front of his family, while on the other side, Bishop Edir Macedo from the Universal Church of the Kingdom of God.

TABLE of CONTENTS

CHAPTER 3 - PARADISE

CHAPTER 1 - PURGATORY

The Rock Bottom is on the 10th Floor

It was a night just like any other for Grigore. After so many failures, he gave up fighting insomnia. The two daily doses of Neozine were more of a habit, since they no longer had a soothing effect.

Grigore knew that the true cure was far away, although the problem was quite near. By his side, Nadege slept or pretended to be sleeping, as she also suffered from chronic insomnia. He had no idea, as they did not speak to each other anymore. The only ways of communication were the constant fights. Thinking about his life was a horrible refuge. Night after night Grigore's thoughts were all about what he called a "familiar curse". In the 50s, his aunt Lívia, his mother's sister, committed suicide. Eight years after that restless night, his mother herself did the same. Around midnight, Tonine Valeriu, known as Nina, went to the window on the 10th floor where she lived and jumped to her death. Grigore looked at his clock: it was a little after midnight and he also lived on the 10th floor.

From the psychiatrists that dealt with his mother schizophrenia, Grigore heard that the disease had hereditable roots, so he carried suicide in his blood.

The simple glance at the large window was a challenge. He concluded that it was time to face his destiny. At that moment, at least the depressive crisis had a hold of his marriage. This was a real crisis, but like his mother, Grigore faced long sad periods without any clear explanation. Tired and sleepless, the idea of suicide that night sounded like a very reasonable argument: Why not? Even aware that this act would torment the lives of his wife and his two small children, the idea sounded like the best alternative for his pain.

However, before getting up, one of the many voices that echoed in his head gave him another suggestion. Grigore remembered the repeated times that his housekeeper suggested listening to Radio Copacabana, which belonged to the Universal Church of the Kingdom of God. For Grigore that was annoying. It was impossible for him, the owner of the house, to pass by the kitchen because the housekeeper would listen to this religious radio all day long. "Orders from the pastor", according to her. Besides, Grigore hated to receive advice from people, especially from his protestant housekeeper who used to listen to the couple's fights through the door gaps.

Another reason for not turning the radio on, a deeper reason: listening to Jesus's name gave him repulsion. Religious speeches were something far too distant from his formation in Romania, where the polity simply had decreed that God did not exist. The spiritual world was a weakness, a deviation, an illusion.

Even with all these arguments, the voice asked him "Why not?", after all, the alternative to that was suicide, so why not give this opportunity a chance?

Grigore turned on the clock radio on the bed table and quickly found the right station, the one he heard a hundred times as he passed by the housekeeper. He paid almost no attention to the words of the pastor that broke the silence in the bedroom. The barrier of skepticism did not allow him to concentrate. Yet, somehow, those words had a more relaxing and weird power than Neozine. After some minutes of speech in different voice tones, many mentions to Jesus Christ and so many others to the Devil, to the Scriptures, and amazing moves to charm the audience, Grigore simply fell asleep. A smooth one like never before.

Radio Terror

It was not the first time that a few instants of radio had provoked outstanding changes in Grigore's life. When he was a fifteen-year-old child in Bucharest, dominated by Communism at that time, he was with his father, Emilian Valeriu, trying to tune into any station just for a distraction. It was difficult considering that most of the stations only divulged official governmental releases.

The broadcasters extolled the success of the polity that contradistinguished with the reality of the country. The Romania that once was a prosperous place now had long lines to buy food — sometimes leftovers. They had heaters that worked only four months out of the year, a rough education that did not allow contestation, and to make things even worse, spies infiltrated the bars, offices, factories, and any place with people, ready to denounce those who complained about the problems of the country. These spies played the role of good guys, always willing to have a good conversation with strangers. The bait was to talk about corruption or cost of living. Whoever took this bait and started complaining would be in trouble. Complaining was a subversive act. Punishment would be prison or shooting.

When Grigore's father turned the knob and heard unfamiliar voices, he got confused. The voices spoke in Romanian but the transmission came from about 1,800 kilometers away in Paris, dissidents of Communism founded Radio Free Europe in order to denounce the abuses in the homeland. Grigore, still a child, did not understand but his father understood he might be in big trouble. He changed stations so no one would accuse him of being dissatisfied.

The discretion was useless. His neighbor also heard the transmission in the apartment next door and, desired to please the polity, denounced Grigore's father. The police came to our house after labeling us as Radio Free Europe's listeners. Grigore and his mother watched as his father tried to explain what happened before being taken to elucidate the situation, which took many days. It was only on the fourth day that Emilian came back dispirited. He was very different from his convivial self.

His family then asked him the inevitable "What happened to you during those three days?" Grigore's father refused to answer. He simply went to his room and did not talk about it for years. Later, during supper, he announced, "We are leaving Romania".

A Pregnant World

Grigore was about to leave the land that molded his multifaceted personality over a period of years, undefined by the world where he was born.

Grigore was conceived and born in a no man's land. On August 23, 1944, a little before Nina Avram got pregnant, Romanian Marshal Ion Ionescu suffered a coup from his debilitated army. United with politicians from the opposing party, the order was for Romania to abandon the Axis Powers and join the Allied Powers. The Nazis were not at all willing to accept this, so the end of the year was a period of much heartache for the Romanians during the war. Anyway, King Mihai's power, of only 23 years, prevailed. In a short time, he went from being a Nazi figurehead to a leader of a coup that would take them down. Four years before, Mihai was a teenager that served the purpose of Ionescu and the Iron Guard, a Nazi organization that obeyed orders from the Führer: to take Romania from neutrality the country held so far and engaged in the war along with Germany, Italy and Japan. The door was open for 500 thousand Nazi troops to take over the country.

Mihai's father, Carol II, went into exile, so under the iron hand of Antonescu, Romania would live out its holocaust. The dictator that grew up under the care of a Jewish stepmother later got married to a French-Jew. He would later exterminate, according to modest estimates, 250 thousand Jews and 25 thousand Gypsies.

Grigore's family knew quite well, what would be expected of the Jewish people like themselves. The hate against the oppressor was prevalent in the streets. Jewish friends, sometimes whole families, were taken by train to their death in the concentration camps. Since escaping was impossible, there was only one way to preserve life: buying it. Grigore's family was rich, and the greed of the Government and Nazi were high. Grigore's grandfather, his mother's father, influence counted. There was an implicit deal between the Nazis and the government to preserve the wealthy. Even with the high numbers of death, Romania was one of the countries in which most of the Jews survived. One of the reasons was due to the large contribution the Jews gave on the economic improvement of the country as of the Constitution of 1923. Romania grew like never before in a decade but this did not stop in the 1930s. Fascist parties emerged on the political scenario and accused the Jews, who were not as successful as the entrepreneurs were, but were responsible for the moral collapse of the country. Still, the most influent families were preserved because they could be useful in the wars in general.

Grigore's grandfather was one of the influent Jews. Max Avram was a man of vision. He knew how to negotiate cogently, from a simple contract to protection for his family. Way before the war, he had realized that Romania would be healthy and prosperous if it kept its factories. The country had always been about agriculture and oil. Therefore, the settlement of the first factories was not an easy job, such as Adesgo, the sock factory. In order to execute his plan, Max went to Germany to convince the local managers to invest in his future dream. He did it. He went back to Bucharest with raw material, equipment and tons of German socks to make. He made money fast. Romania kept essentially rural, but Max Avram opened a new class of industrial men.

His daughter was, therefore, one of the best brides a young Romanian man could have. Young, beautiful and classy, Tonine Avram enjoyed dreaming about Hollywood movies. She preferred the ones with a charming man, with a seductive smile and green eyes that Americans loved up to his death. Frank Sinatra started to emerge in movies like Higher and Higher and Swooner Crooner as a guy who was making the hearts of women all over the world beat faster. Nina was one of these women.

For that reason, among many of her suitors, one that aroused her feelings was Emilian Herscovici. He was not the richest person; however, he was from an influent family, but maybe not the most reliable. He had come from the countryside to study in Bucharest and was delighted with the free and uncompromising lifestyle, with a whole world and many women to conquer. The dazzle lasted his entire life, but at that time, Nina still did not know it. She did not even care. What mattered to her was that he was just like Frank Sinatra. In addition to his green eyes, he was classy, and had a smile that could be an enigma: he could be that man who offered warming arms or a scoundrel that could vanish at any time. He was the chosen one.

They had a marriage everybody heard about. The photographs at that time revealed luxury and attention to details. Most of the GDP of Romania was present.

Sometime later, Nina got pregnant. The family's concerns were hugh – not because of the unwanted pregnancy, but because Nazism was still around. Adults still could not get used to the precarious balance between negotiating with the devil and preventing the future. Besides, there was another reason that made surviving at that time grueling. Grigore's parents – with the support of the rest of the family – helped Allied soldiers. The ones who passed through Bucharest in order to fight Hitler and the SS found among the Hercovicis protection, shelter, clothing and food, as well as other valuable information. After the war, they earned a special decoration by the English Supreme Commander H. R. Alexander, of "gratitude and esteem for the help given to the sailors, soldiers and members of English Aviation". However, at that time, this act could be the end for any of whoever helped. Before such a nebulous horizon, the family reunited to decide what to do with their upcoming baby. Emilian's sister, Valéria, found the perfect metaphor: such as Moses, who was in a basket along the Nile River for survival, the baby had to hide his identity as a Jew. The Hercovicis physiognomy made the task easier: they did not look Jewish. The tradition of circumcision could be abolished for a greater good. They had to erase the marks of Judaism from their identity.

The first was a name change for his mother. Since Sinatra's double was hers, to the baby she reserved the name of another Hollywood star. Grigore was the chosen name, after Gregory Peck but with the second syllable stressed. For that reason, the change of I in the beginning and e in the end, the way it was written in Romania. As his family name, her mother's name, Avram, which although referring to the patriarch of Jewish people, Agraham was also a common last name even among non-Jew Romanians. In the end, a second last name was developed at that time: Valeriu, after Aunt Valéria, the savior.

When Grigore was born, nine months later, the world was different. Nazism was losing ground. They lost their leader, Adolf Hitler, who committed suicide in 1945. On May 7, 1945, Germany surrendered, which marked a victory for the Allies.

Grigore came into this world on July 21, 1945. At that time, Europe was being divided. In the West was the advance of the American and English troops. In the East, the Soviet Union took the territories once belonging to the Nazi. The world was divided into two blocks – capitalist and socialist – and Grigore was in the second one. Officially, Romania only became the Communist People's Republic in 1947, but before that the Red Army became a reality in the country, calling the shots.

The year of Grigore's birth, decisive in the history of humanity, was not over. On the global confrontation, the shocking moment was on August 6 and 9, when the USA bombed the Japanese cities of Hiroshima and Nagasaki

On the private confrontation that would be Grigore's future life, there was an amazing coincidence. One, which would be the darker character of his deeper journey in 1945. On January 18, 1946, the future Bishop Edir Macedo was born.

Hitler out, Stalin in

On the first days of the after war, the Romanians reacted euphorically and perceived the Soviets as their rescuers that finally arrived. The war had ended, hope for freedom and prosperity was in the air once again. However, there were people who diverged from this optimism. Max Avram was one of them. His vision about the Communists was one of distrust. What should have been worrisome, since he was a man of vision?

The fact is that Max did not wait to see if his thoughts were right. He soon announced to his family his decision to leave Romania. The Communist Command still tried to manage the legacy of the Nazi Party and put order to the chaos of the country. During its first years, the new government did not care who left the country. Utilizing these open frontiers, Max sold his sock factory in one of the worst transactions of history, since nobody had money Asdego went to a new owner for a very low price. The little money he made with the transaction was enough for him to leave for Germany with his wife Minca. In general, the Romanians that emigrated at that time had as their destiny Yugoslavia, which offered advantages such as being close to Romania and a capitalist country. However, the couple chose Germany, where they imagined they'd find lost prosperity. Once again, Max was right. In Germany, he built another factory and became even richer and more influent. On a tragic note, Max underwent an unsuccessful prostate operation, which took his life. His wife Minca and his daughter Lívia immigrated to Israel.

Their decision was wise. As soon as the Communist Government organized, the second act of the tragedy started for the Romanians. The first extreme step was about the Socialist ideals: no citizen should own anything. Now, everything belonged to the Government. Farms, lands, apartments, bank accounts and factories – and between them, Adesgo, whose owner was now far from Romania. This country, which once belonged to both rich and poor people, now had only poor citizens. Out of the blue, due to the decrees of the new

Government, Romania became a society with no classes.

The exception was the Government itself, which became the only administrative and financial elite of the country. If Romanians had a voucher to buy staples and food in long lines at supermarkets, members of the Communist Party created markets that only them could frequent. Their food was imported. Even though Romania was strong agriculturally, they could not even sustain themselves. The country had become the backyard of the Soviet Union. What was produced went to the matrix in order to enrich and empower the USSR against the USA. To Romanians go the leftovers, while the red elite enjoy the imported goods.

It was not unusual to find in the streets, the Romanians who missed Nazism. On the occupation level, the ones who were not victims of the holocaust took their lives with more or less freedom, but with no poverty. Romania was a rich country. It was said, that they had the same lifestyle, culture and prosperity of France. Therefore, there was a saying that if it rained in Paris, umbrellas would open in Bucharest.

In communism, misery took over the country. If bread was expensive, freedom was even rarer. The new Government realized that soon Romania would lose its citizens, so it closed the doors for the ones intending to leave the country. Emigration was impossible.

People were forced, not only to remain in the country but also to think that this was the right decision, at least in public. Spies were everywhere, ready to denounce dissatisfied citizens. The old habit of sitting, drinking, and talking bad about the Government could put a person in jail. The unwary one who got distracted – by revolt or for drinking too much – and started complaining would also go in jail.

The tragic element is that five years before one could not prevent what the future awaited. The war was over, The Nazi were defeated, and so optimism reigned, excepting some citizens with more experience of life, such as Grigore's grandfather, who left the country as soon as they could. The remaining ones enjoyed their old lifestyle for a while. Communism organized its dictatorship, closing down the frontiers, nationalizing the goods of the population, establishing censorship, and planning the economy in this time.

To Grigore's family, the transformation became clearer when a family came to live in their house. Because of Communism, each family had the right to a specific square meters for each person to live, and the Valerius, with their huge apartment, was a building with two apartments on each floor. Therefore, they had to live with strangers.

That was the last knockout of a series at the fortune they had gathered. They no longer had their factory, the money they saved now belonged to the Estate, and finally, the apartment had to be shared. Only the family jewels remained, which Grigore's mother was able to hide at the bottom of the wardrobe cabinet. That was the heritage that the family had, characterizing what would be his first fast passage from wealth into poverty in Grigore's life — something he would relive many other times in the future.

In a short time of living with the new inhabitants, things became unbearable. Sharing living quarters might work pretty well in the spreadsheets of bureaucrats who organized the economy, but it was a catastrophe when put into practice. Living together became impossible until the Valerius chose to live in another place, still keeping the square meters they had the right to. After a few days of searching, they found a small kitchenette. It was tiny, but it was theirs.

The place was so small that there was not a place for the refrigerator — a luxury product, only found in the homes of communist tycoons. The solution was to improvise a small wooden crate — as a mini ambry — and solder it outside the window, with the risk it would fall onto someone's head. Bucharest's cold was responsible to keep food colder than if they were inside a refrigerator. If someone needed to get something, they would have to open the window, remove all the ice layers and then reach for what they wanted. This was a really hard task because of the cold and the Government, which limited the operation of heaters.

Grigore's childhood lived on both sides of the street in the new polity. During the first years, it was great because of what money could buy. Even the games he played were a reflection of that changing. When the poorest and richest people were still around, Grigore enjoyed something that not everybody could afford, thus revealing an inclination toward business. His bicycle was his own private property, which was still allowed but was also his capital to generate benefits. Because other boys were keen to ride it, Grigore charged them a high price for a ride on his bicycle. When it was time to spend his money, he revealed his other face as a businessmen: he was extremely tightfisted. He used to bargain for better prices at fruit stands, buying the overripe ones for less.

Later, when he lived at the kitchenette, even buying overripe fruits was not easy. The game had changed. During the afternoons, the kids who liked cars would gather around the window and dream. They dreamt that the first car to pass by would belong to one of them, the second to someone else and so on. They would take into consideration the brand, year, cost and condition, so at the end of the day, they would calculate who made the best profits. It was a game that would take the whole afternoon because few cars were driven on the streets of Bucharest, the effect of an economy, which invested more in the industry and less in consumer goods. Very few people had cars, and the automobiles were not very good. After cheering for more cars to appear, the kids had to be content with the little *money* they made.

Another talent that appeared at a young age was to advocate. Grigore would use the same abilities of persuasion that he used in his businesses when saving someone's life. Once he spent the whole morning playing soccer – another of his passions – with the other kids on the street. At lunchtime, his mother, stricter than his father – unlike Emilian, who had never spanked Grigore, Tonine now and then used the pedagogical recourse of spanking – called him once, twice and Grigore did not pay attention. Once again, she called, but no response. In the middle of the afternoon Grigore showed up in front of the apartment and his mother ordered him to go upstairs. He started negotiating. He said he would only go up if she promised not to spank him. The response "we will talk when you're up here" did not convince him. His mother promised him nothing would happen but that was not enough. Suspicious, Grigore recognized false promises. Because the whole discussion was being screamed – he was downstairs and she on the fourth floor – Grigore had the great idea of inviting witnesses. He called his neighbors to participate in the trial and checked if all of them had heard what his mother promised. The neighbors witnessed in his favor and only then Grigore went back home. This method was good but Grigore learned that justice did not always prevail. Without worrying about breaking her promise, Grigore's mother spanked him like never before with a broomstick.

Of course, scolding was an exception, and Grigore's parents were far from being violent people. On the contrary, the strictest moments were a lesson to counterbalance all the caring he received for being an only child.

During one of their vacations, usually on the beach, Grigore's parents were warned by the doctor, their son had appendicitis with a forty degree Celsius fever. He was delusional and required medical attention.

On the same night, they took the first train back home. They were in such a hurry that at the station, with the train leaving, Emilian threw himself inside the car but did not realize his wife was not able to do so. The solution was to pull her through the window.

When they arrived home, they found Grigore jumping and having fun. The crisis had ended, the fever was gone. With the end of the panic, Grigore's parents scolded him. A scolding Grigore could not understand then but understood now. He was scolded for being healthy and ruining their vacation.

Atheist by Decree

When Grigore entered school, Communism was an official subject. The evaluation he makes about the impact of that education on his personality has two sides, a positive and a negative one. The positive side is the strict discipline of which he was subjected. Times were strict – not even five minutes late were allowed –, absents were not tolerated and children soon learned how to respect authority.

There was the other side of the coin, of course. Respect also meant the total impossibility of disagreement. Questioning was forbidden. The only time Grigore tried to do so, he had his hair cut as punishment. The official truth was absolute. To assure that, the school was in charge to reproduce the fear that surrounded the streets. It was not the case of training spy kids or plea-bargaining, but if inspectors, principals of teachers, noticed any contestation attitude, the punishment would happen. Grigore knew them all since he could not help making jokes about the teachers with his friends.

The Communist world impregnated all classes, especially history. Romania was the country that finally got rid of domination, while unconscionable capitalists who got rich inhabited the west by the hunger and misery of others.

Regarding spiritual education, teaching was one: God does not exist. End of story. There were no religion classes, nor reference to Jesus Christ or Christianity whatsoever. Teachers who talked about it only said that God was an invention of Capitalism, and religion was a silly idea. To Grigore, it was not too hard to adapt to that idea. Despite being Jewish, his family did not follow the traditions. His maternal grandparents – for Grigore they had already been dead – they were connected to religion. His parents, however, especially when Communism frowned upon religious practices, abandoned Judaism.

However, it was unpleasant being forced to spend Christmas at school. One of the strongest traditions in Romania was Sorcova. In the country, the Orthodox religion prevailed. On Christmas, Jesus' birthday was celebrated with the whole family the night before, like in Brazil and many other countries. On December 24, from dawn to dusk, Romanian kids would go out in the streets knocking on everyone's door singing a Christmas carol which started with the word Sorcova, which meant a flower crown, with which kids blessed the listeners. In exchange, they would earn sweets, panettones, gifts and sometimes some money.

Grigore participated in some Sorcovas before getting into school. On a very successful day – when he was six –, he arrived home at night with his pockets full of money. He was dragging them with difficulty from the panettones. He expected joy from everybody for his profit, but instead, for the first time in his life, his father slapped him in the face. Grigore was good at convincing people to make donations, but he left the house in the morning and stayed out the whole day without telling anyone where he was.

The fact is that Sorcova was a rooted tradition and the polity must have thought that it could be bad for marketing to put tanks outside to repress the kids. The solution was to promote Christmas parties in school – without saying that it was a celebration since that was a Capitalist thing. The party would happen during the whole day, being mandatory and with closed doors. The polity banned outside games but isolated everybody on the inside, so they would not have any affiliation with Christmas.

It was a within-the-wall event and completely lame. The attendance was mandatory. The impossibility of getting out of the event did not make it fun. Anyway, Sorcova lost ground and the idea did not work out. Over the years, God and Jesus were not spoken of in Romania.

For Grigore, this education offered great results. He not only did not believe in God but also felt repulsion to the name of Jesus Christ.

It took him some time to adapt to school. He walked there every morning for 15 minutes. In the beginning, he was a little standoffish. He was afraid of being called to the blackboard and when that happened, jitters made him mess up all of the answers. Therefore, at the end of the first year, which he feared the worst, at the final event, which gathered parents and teachers to discuss the students' development, Grigore was sure he would be among the ones who failed the year. That is why he chose radical measures: he simply did not invite his parents.

He missed a great moment. His name was announced by the principal, not amongst the ones who had failed, but amongst the ones that excelled. His mother missed this glorious moment.

From that day on, Grigore started believing in himself and started to blossom at another of his main characteristics: be the best at what he did. He would stand out for all the other years as well, which would cost him a ticket to a better school. At this new school, among his classmates were Nicolau Ceausescu's daughter, a dictator, and still minister.

However, Grigore did not care about dictatorship, even though the topic was about to be decisive for his family.

The Cost of Freedom

In 1962, the capture of Emilian Valeriu by the police was enough to make him decide to abandon the country as soon as possible. Only 3 years later his classmate's father would take over after Gheorghiu, the dictator at that time, who died. If repression was unbearable for the Valerius, things were about to get worse. Ceausescu would govern Romania during 24 years under genocides and a cult to personality inspired by Kim Il-Sung, leader of North Korea. After making himself *Conducator* (boss), Ceausescu made the last worker sweat in order to build the Parliament Palace, the second tallest building in the world, to match the grandiosity of its dictator.

In Romania, people would see the end of Communism, which would spread all over Eastern Europe by the end of the 80s. The army, which had orders from the dictator to repulse a protest in Timisoara City, affiliated with the protesters. Ceausescu ran away with his wife on a helicopter but was captured after the pilot landed due to technical issues. The days later, Ceausescu and Elena were shot in public.

The Valerius were not at all interested in staying to check what the future reserved for their country. The problem was that leaving was not only about wanting to. When Grigore's father announced the family would leave Romania, the question was simple: how? The polity was completely established and vigilant, to the point of detecting as subversive any citizen who would listen to a resistance radio channel for less than one minute at his own home. The exit was closed.

The solution was to contact their relatives in Israel. After the exit of Grigore's grandparents, their aunts by father, Valeria, and Melanie abandoned Romania and recover the influence and prosperity in Tel-Aviv. Emilian and Tonine would appeal to them since Max Avram had passed after a delicate surgery to remove a prostate cancer in the late 50s.

That was the same solution used during Nazism to protect the life of the Hescovicis: influence. The Communist government needed money. The deal was for 2 thousand dollars. The bureaucracy that followed was a result not of the cost, but of the red prudency. The Communist staff did not simply want to receive bribery and open the gates. In order to make things seem legal, a contract established between England and Romania was smuggled. This contract was about cattle sales and had an additional clause that allowed Israelites to withdraw their relatives from Romania by an established cost. After two months of bureaucrat pending, the contract was finally signed. Emilian, Nina and Grigore did not waste time and went to the airport to take a plane and go to Paris.

One of the conditions for a citizen to be able to leave the country was that they can leave, but their goods must stay. It was completely forbidden to emigrate with any goods at all. In the kitchenette, their last belongings were left behind.

Not happy about reaching that moment in life with nothing, Nina decided to take risks. She decided to hide some family jewels inside her underwear. The jewels, which survived the polity, would pass another test. She would be searched at the airport, but Grigore's parents were pretty sure that a 43-year-old woman would pass without having her private parts searched.

The police searched the entire family. Mother and father were separated and searched separately. The father was released and sent inside the plane with Grigore, without news about her wife. The flight attendant asked the passengers to take their seats and fasten their seat belts, and even the despair of Grigore and his father did not use. No information. Getting off the airplane was impossible. They had to travel separated from Nina and with the torment of leaving her with the Romanian police.

Nina had the opportunity of living one of the scenes that made her cry when watching movies. At the last moment, the flight procedure had to be changed and the doors, which were already close, opened up. Nina was able to board in time to be with her family, in tears.

Not even a hero, classic figure in action movies, was out in this story. Later in Paris Nina would tell that the police, in fact, did find the jewels and stopped her from boarding. She was being arrested, until an officer who was in charge decided to give her back the jewels and ordered her to board the plane. The Valerius would never forget this.

In Paris, his father finally told them what happened when the police held him for three days in Bucharest. Only there Emilian could do that because the last series of threats he made was not to tell anyone what happened, which was part of a psychological torture. He was locked in a small cell, each time he was subjected to a new interrogation. The objective was to force him into confessing a connection with the rebels. Nothing convinced the opposition that Emilian was just randomly dialing his radio when he tuned to Radio Free Europe. The police felt threatened by his perspicacity and started beating him up. This situation happened for three days. Because nothing was said, they sent him home, but with a notice.

From Paris, Israel was the destination. Aunt Valeria and now the savior Aunt Melanie, who had paid the two thousand dollars to the communists, were waiting for a better life. Besides, they were Jews, who finally found a place to live in peace. Emilian even had a job as a taxi driver waiting for him. Nothing was more natural than to end their journey in Tel-Aviv.

The annoyance to all of this came from where they would never guess. Young Grigore, then in his 17 years of age, protested. He did not exactly know why, but he was incisive when he said he did not want to move to Israel. What at first seemed like a whim, had turned into a very delicate familiar crisis. Grigore was sure that if his parents wanted to go, they could. He saw his future in other lands. When asked what land, he quickly responded: Brazil.

Coffee and Pelé: Visions of Paradise

Why Brazil? That was a hard question to answer. Grigore's decision was a mix of intuition with practicality and scattered information. In this last topic, it was all about the same information all foreigners have about Brazil. At that time all news that arrived in Europe was about how strong Brazil was in soccer. Brazil had just won its second World Cup. Four years later, it was the only team that had won outside of his continent, in Sweden. Grigore – already crazy about soccer – followed everything through the news. He dreamed about being among the best players in the world.

Grigore wanted to live in Brazil, even though he did not know why. Nowadays he sees his choice as heaven providence, a divine whisper "I did not know how to explain to my parents, I just knew I had to come to Brazil", said Grigore. With more information than his fellow countrymen, he knew that besides soccer, Brazil exported coffee. That world where Pelé and coffee coexisted seemed like a happy, harmonious hopeful place, like Heaven on earth. Grigore kept his will alive. He used his argumentative powers and convinced his parents. Emilian and Nina would never live in Israel. Their future lied on the other side of the Atlantic Ocean.

The ship voyage lasted 17 days. From Paris, they went to Napoli by train, where they navigated Corrientes River in Argentina. On the way to Buenos Aires, there were stops in Spain, Portugal, Madeira Island and Rio de Janeiro. In Portuguese cities, the tourists – most Italians who would visit America – got off to shop, and to appreciate the beautiful places. Grigore and his parents could not enjoy like the others. Portugal lived under the regime of the dictator Antonio Salazar, who in the past flirted with Fascism. People who were getting away from

Communism were not welcome at all. Getting off the ship could result in being arrested.

Staying on the ship was not comfortable. The small cabin they were sharing was in the basement. When it rained, they all got sick, but nothing compared to the storm that hit the ship. Inside the cabin, Grigore and his parents were thrown against the walls, and if they looked out the window, they would be sure the ship was sinking. The sea already covered the basement of the ship, so they could see the fish through the cabin window.

The confinement was over when they saw Guanabara's Bay. From the ship, the typical postcard image was perfect. The undertow creates dunes on the beach, which invaded Atlântica Avenue, making it hard for Beetles, Gordinis and a couple of Simca Chambord, which were driven in Rio. It was a holiday, October 12, and the Cariocas were out. This was a new world, far from wars – Nazism or Cold War. They were both traumatic experiences to the Valerius, so they were happy for being really far from the world's conflicts.

The cars on the streets were a sign of a country that was changing. Brazil was living the development euphoria of JK years, followed by the depression of the election and resignation of Jânio Quadros, and now a political and economic intermezzo. From 1957 to 1960, industrialization expected at the Goals Plan of President Juscelino Kubitschek made the country produce 321,000 cars, 90% more than expected. From the first cars entirely manufactured in Brazil, Romiseta in 1955, with the debut of Rural Willys, and the entrance of the big car manufacturers, the 1960 industry manufactured 6,124 Aero-Willys, 3,633 Simca Chambords, and 11,299 Kombis. The Gross National Product grew 7.9% a year, against 5.2% in the five previous years because of foreign investors that added $2.2 million Dollars from 1955 until 1961.

The investments were also made to the roads, air transportation, electricity and steel. Brazil grew and became urbanized, but foreign debt and inflation jumped from 19.2% in 1956 to 30.9% in 1960, shaking the optimism of the 50 years in five proposed by JK.

After a political phenomenon that, with a broom, promised to sweep the masses, but that lasted just a little – Jânio only ruled the country for 7 months and 25 days – Brazil had an impasse. The country was divided between the ones who did not want to see the vice-president João Goulart take over and the ones who defended the maintenance of the constitutional order. The solution was in between both of these. A Congress commission approved the parliament, so Goulart could become president, but with his hand tied not to put into practice, his base reforms, which intended to "defend economic order against certain misuses which compromised the true national behalf". In 1962, when Grigore arrived, the nation awaited the referendum scheduled for January of the following year to decide which side Brazil would take: the return of the Presidential System and all the fuss of a president from the Left Party would bring or the maintenance of the interim solution until new elections. The first hypothesis won.

To Grigore, all was ok with the country. Brazil met the expectations. Leme Beach, where he would go every afternoon, had no lines or food shortage. Also, the beauties of Rio and the euphoria of winning the World Cup: Brazil was a paradise. The one thing Grigore had to do now that he was in Brazil was to go to Maracanã and watch a game with the heroes of ginga, dribble and creativity. Grigore was able to see Amarildo, the captain of the squad Nilton Santos, Zagallo, and Garrincha, who was even better than he imagined. Only Didi was not playing that day since he was traded after the World Cup. It was an unforgivable day despite the sad result. Botafogo started winning the game 2 - 0 against the International Porto Alegre but ended up losing the rhythm and drawing the game.

Not long after through the contacts of Uncle Leopoldo, Grigore's father got him a job at his Emerson Televisions factory. Uncle Leopoldo was not a blood relative, but he had great influence. In Europe, Emilian's little sister, Irina, became sister-in-law of the most famous writer of Western Germany, Helena Feigl. Her daughter Melanie became consul and ambassadress of Israel. Aunt Valeria had as her brother-in-law a member of the Romanian Government, Leopoldo Stern. If in the past, Stern had contributed with the Hercovicis to preserve Nazism, now his influence was still valuable. After the war, Stern was one to leave Romania and started making a fortune in other places. First in the USA, then in Brazil. In Brazil, among his many investments, he bought an entire building in Laranjeiras, a district in Rio, rented all the apartments and started living on the income. One of his sons was Uncle Leopoldo, who since the beginning, followed his father's ways and started buying and renting apartments. He soon would have substantial income and no longer needed to work.

The other daughter of Stern got married in Romania to a brilliant lawyer named Felix Klein. A friend from the drinking sprees of Emilian Hercovici, Klein was the type who left in the early hours of the day to defend a case in the morning without knowing the details and would win the case. He would obtain a visa to Brazil, which was only possible at that time if the immigrant was assured a job. No problem: Klein got a place for his friend in Emerson and later in the Vespa scooter factory. Klein was friends with the owner of Vespa, and that was a big deal. During that time scooters were in fashion throughout the streets of Rio de Janeiro, and later, when the Lambretta came along and surpassed Vespa, the owner Sammy Kohn decided to do other things, such as open a bank and get funding from England to build the Rio-Niterói Bridge.

Klein himself decided before, that during the 50s, he would try his luck in Brazil. Here he met another Romanian, Alfredo Monteverde, who had just received a bulky inheritance from his millionaire father and did not know what to do with the money. Then they started to import refrigerators from the United States, which were still rare here. He opened a shop called Ponto Frio. They sold at an alarming rate. The refrigerator that started the decade in only 11.6% of Brazilian homes had achieved a level of 26% by 1970. This is in comparison to the almost 90% level of today. This was a growth of 126% which gave the new entrepreneurs' face a smile for years. Klein was the director and right-hand man of Monteverde, a guy so schizophrenic that his private car was an ambulance. Anywhere he went his driver used the white van completely equipped with the best medicine for any emergency. Just like every other hypochondriac, one day Montenegro passed away. Klein, as a lawyer, helped his wife in a judicial battle for the rights of Ponto Frio against Montenegro's mother, married to Raymond Safra, owner of the homonymous bank. In addition, he won, taking as a benefit the job of permanent director of Ponto Frio.

In all that, we see good fortune following the nucleus of the successful Jews gravitating around the Hercovicis in Romania and coming to Brazil. Emilian, Nina and Grigore had near them persons who were embodying the economic transformation era in this country.

In addition to such huge support, the Valerius also counted with an institution that helped Jewish immigrants. They not only paid their tickets but also funded their first months for the family in Rio de Janeiro until they managed to get on their feet. Other invaluable help: the Portuguese's course. He was feeling desperate for living in paradise but not being able to talk with anyone. He walked on the sidewalk of Atlântica Avenue trying to decipher the sounds around him and nothing. Sometimes he would buy a newspaper and try to read it, always in vain. His tragic situation sometimes was also funny. On one particular day, his mother asked him to go to the corner shop and buy butter. Grigore told her did not know how to say butter. The mother, after thinking a little, concluded it should be the same way they asked for it during breakfast on the ship. Grigore went out to do the errand.

At the corner shop, he asked the man behind the balcony exactly as he learned. "I want a *burro*." "Burro" is butter in Italian, the language most spoken by a person on a ship leaving Napoli. However, in Portuguese "*burro*" means "stupid". The owner of the corner shop couldn't understand so Grigore started to speak louder:

Stupid, stupid! The man got angry, not only due to his tone but because – for a supreme bad luck – he was Portuguese, and even understanding that in Brazil it was common to tell jokes portraying Portuguese people as stupid, he thought that an innocent lad entering his shop to offend him was off of limits. Grigore couldn't understand the fury of the Portuguese man because of such a simple request for butter, and fortunately, when things were starting to get bad, he saw a packet of what he wanted on the shelf and started to point decidedly, as if saying "this is the stupid!" The owner sold it to him. However, asking himself if that boy was really foreign or merely a more innocent lad from Rio de Janeiro.

Gradually the language and the lifestyle were coming together. In Vespa, Emilian started as a distributor and soon became a director. Grigore entered high school in the Anglo-Americano school. The obvious educational gap was as large as the gap between him and his colleagues. The High school education he received here was equivalent to the subjects Grigore studied in Bucharest's secondary school. He was so upset that at any given time he could not hold it in any longer. From his chair, he reprimanded the teacher, saying aloud he was wrong. The drama is that Grigore said the sentence wrong in Portuguese, and instead of the teacher being corrected, he was the one being mocked by his colleagues.

The following year he would go to Vetor School, which prepared students for the college entrance exam. Far from being a popular kid, he tried to have fun when he was not studying. He walked onto the beach of Lemo where he used to play racquetball. He didn't risk playing soccer. In addition, the problem was not only his lack of ability to make new friendships, but he lacked the agility to play soccer on the sands of this world championship country.

The Fall

In Rio, Emilian Valeriu had what it took to become the Frank Sinatra of the tropics. This was the role that suited him the best. One would say, because of his gentle nature, communicative skills and good manners he blended better with the face of Rio de Janeiro more so than back in his native Eastern Europe. For that very reason, it must have been extremely hard for a person who liked to talk to not understand what everyone else was saying. Being 58 years old, he had little inclination to learn another language, so he was limited to the basics and to coexist with Leopoldo, Klein and a few other Romanians who lived in Brazil. Relationships outside of the marriage were also becoming very laborious.

Without many options, he poured himself into his work, which brought him constant recognition due to his professional capability.

One outstanding aspect of Emilian's personality was his willingness to help people. In the family, he was the one prepared to face the food line from which they did not manage to get free. Every day, around 5 a.m., a battalion of housewives left their homes with glass bottles to fill them from the carts carrying drums of milk. There was a milk supply crisis, and those carts, stationed away in rather distant corners of the city, were the way to bypass it.

Emilian played the role of a housewife by ensuring there was milk on the breakfast table for his family every morning. A widow of Romanian origin, an aunt of Leopold Stern, was counting on the fact that Emilian would take milk to her every morning. A favor he performed every day with pleasure.

One given morning, even delayed by his job at Vespa, he did not want to leave the old lady without her bottle of milk. In a hurry, he crossed Princess Isabel Avenue without paying attention. A driver couldn't avoid him and ended up hitting Emilian, throwing him towards the sidewalk, where he hit his head. Grigore's father was unconscious but alive. However, the blood loss seen by the pedestrians and drivers showed the seriousness of the situation.

Grigore and a work colleague of his fathers' found Emilian in the public hospital at Miguel Couto. The first two actions were transferring him to the renowned Beneficiência Portuguesa hospital and then to hide this from his mother, until they had more information.

Tonine had fragile nerves. For a long time in Romania, she was diagnosed with a disease that astonished the family: schizophrenia. She was hospitalized on several occasions during moments of crisis. Her emotional state was cyclical, alternating between moments of depression and paranoia traces. A renowned German psychiatrist, Gunther Freud, treated Nina. Even with the status of his surname and training that was able to solve and cure the human soul; Freud could do little for Nina. All that was within his reach was writing prescriptions, typical for medical doctors of the time: very strong pills that took the patient out of the schizophrenia but threw her into depression, with the appearance of being drugged. The family's only safe port for Nina Valeriu – that due to the health problems felt much more the difficulties for adaptation – and Grigore was afraid, with reason. The shock due to the accident of his father would be too much for his mother.

In the hospital, Emilian underwent complex surgery on his brain by the best surgeon at the time. He survived, but was still hanging between life and death.

This was the situation Grigore had to report to his mother at the end of the day. Tonine had a serious nervous crisis and they had to call a psychiatrist. The familiar drama was aggravated.

Grigore spent entire days at the hospital. Several days after the accident, Emilian had to undergo yet another operation. That November of 1963 would be a month of extreme anguish for the Valerius, moreover, not only for them but for others as well. On November 22nd, the world watched on TV one of the most brutal murders in history. During an open car parade in Dallas, while waving to the crowd, at the beginning of his campaign for re-election, American president John F. Kennedy was shot in the neck and in the head, collapsing into the lap of his wife Jaqueline.

It would be a day remembered for a lifetime by Grigore and his family. However, in their case, this was not due to the tragedy in the world, but due to their particular tragedy. A few days after Kennedy's murder, Grigore's father died.

Full Pockets, Empty Heart

The destiny of the other two members of his family took opposite courses. The shock from the death of his father pushed Grigore forward into life, one of personal growth. It was during this time he started college and life as a professional.

Meanwhile, his mother was under a force pulling her further into the darkness. The crises of the illness became worse and more frequent. One piece of advice from her psychiatric treatment was to practice activities that made her feel useful. Nina found this chance in an institution called O Pequeno Jornaleiro (The Little News Vendor). In addition to helping herself, the social work still counted with the advantage of helping people. The former first lady of the country, Darcy Vargas, had created the entity and now her daughter with the president, Alzira Vargas, administered it. O Pequeno Jornaleiro was a place where street children received food, direction, proper hygiene and education; in exchange, they sold newspapers in the streets. It was a time in which boys were still competing for the sale of morning papers with the newsstands. This figure of the street boy announcing the daily news was symbolized in a statue that inspired the name of Alzira's institution. Located at the triangle of the streets Ouvidor, Rio Branco and Miguel Couto, with "the open mouth shouting his eternal headline", in the words of Millôr Fernandez. Years later, in 2002, written in the column of journalist Ricardo Boechat, in the diary O Globo was a warning that the statue had disappeared. The first conclusion of the natives of Rio de

Janeiro was that it had been stolen, a symptom of a city where street boys, instead of selling newspapers, were handed to God doing things much worse. However, it was a false alarm: the Little News Vendor statute was moved to the street Sete de Setembro, where it remains today.

In 1963, many people were contributing to the philanthropic entity O Pequeno Jornaleiro, making crochet items, clothes and things in general for sale. Their earnings, summed up to that from the work of the boys, allowed the institution to operate for many long years.

Alzira Vargas also helped people nearby in need. Solidary with Nina's history, she knew that the family in addition to their emotional shock was going through financial problems. Vespa had paid the high expenses of the hospital and, although they were not collecting, Grigore and his mother knew they would have a debt to pay eventually. On the other hand, the family was at an impasse: that same Vespa was provident in contracting a life insurance for his director. But as the value was quite high, the bureaucratic process was looking quite long. The solution came from Alzira. She used her influence – and that of whom more she knew in the society – with the insurance company. Soon the 15 million cruzeiros were received – a great amount of money at the time, around 80 thousand dollars today – to Nina, and they both got breathing space and great solidarity in those mourning times.

Work was occupying the time and the mind of Grigore's mother, avoiding that she ended up going into depression. Emotionally, he got even more attached to her son, in a relation that soon stopped being simply love to becoming absolute dependence. In addition to this role, Grigore had to take another one. Now he was the man in the house. He had to set aside his afternoons at the beach and get an education in life. In summary, he had to grow.

Grigore had no friends to talk to and unburden himself. He still felt like the foreigner, the guy from abroad, with difficulties in communicating because of his shyness powered by the fact that he still was not fluent in Portuguese. When, he used to walk alone, on the beach or on the sidewalk, he observed the groups, the beauty of the natives of Rio de Janeiro and felt resentment of not being a part of their social life. He was really troubled by the fact that he was almost 20 years old and never had a girlfriend.

Even facing the trials and tribulations of poverty in Romania, the prisoning of his father, their escape from the country and the tragic recent loss, Grigore did not find consolation in religion. He remained an atheist as he had become in

Bucharest. He was not fond of psychological and much less religious investigations. On the contrary, he knew that he had to act.

With the life insurance money, he decided to go to college. In addition, he decided to fulfill the dream that his father never achieved. Emilian, since he was a boy, had shown the desire of being an engineer, but somewhere between his intentions and the facts, there was always a gap. Engineering was a difficult career in Romania, one of the most demanding, and considering that Emilian was never a hard-working student, he gave up this dream and became a lawyer. However, he never ceased to mention during talks at dinner that what he wanted to be was an engineer.

Grigore took the entrance exam for engineering and was accepted by two colleges. One was private, PUC, and one was free, the Federal University. What weighed in the choice was not only the value of the monthly payment, but the fact that the Federal University course was quicker: 4 years against 6 in PUC. He then started to take the boat crossing from Rio to Niterói and spend the day studying. He wanted, once again, the best in what he was doing.

During his second year, the students had to choose which major they would follow. The trend at the time was electrical engineering. The national public power company Eletrobrás was just formed, the country was entering a growth phase in the development of electric power. Job-wise, there were more positions than candidates. Eletrobrás was contracting inside the college to assure qualified labor for the promising future. Grigore went with the trend. If unemployment was zero, if all colleagues opted for the electric segment, then it was decided.

The issue is that he never liked to even change a lamp. He realized it had nothing to do with him as quickly as he had made the choice. In the very first semester, he saw he was in a strange world. Then he was radical: he did not want to continue. He left college and tried to find what he wanted in life.

This was a problem: Grigore had no idea what he wanted in life. And since he did not know where to row, the boat of his life drifted. In this situation, the option that appeared was always the best choice. Once again, the Jewish immigrants who came from Romania were solidary. Isidor Schangler, owner of a company called Demolições Demaco, was glimpsing a good future in the company he constituted with the financial backing of other Romanian Jews. Schangler demolished so the partners could construct and sell buildings. Grigore was called to be a business manager. It was time to work.

The job, in addition to bringing growth, also brought something very valuable. Grigore started to feel the emotion of earning his own money. It was not a fortune, but it was more than he needed. Especially because he had adopted a frugal way of life, without unnecessary expenses – and the list of what he needed was quite strict. He didn't buy clothes, he didn't go to parties, nor did he go to dinner or lunch. At the end of each month, by most accounts, he saved most of his wages. Grigore liked to save more and more to be able to invest. He wanted to be rich soon. He bought some shares, but his main investment focus was real estate, following the steps of uncle Leopoldo. Soon he bought his first apartment and, not much later, another one larger, with three rooms, in Lene.

In addition to his effort, he also counted on his wisdom and foresight, much the same as his grandfather. The shares Grigore kept benefited him years later after the *boom* of the Brazilian Stock Exchange near the end of 1970 and beginning of 1971. Grigore's investment yielded a four hundred percent increase.

In addition to the real estate he began to accumulate and his compulsion for saving, he was yet another Hercovici attaining wealth, although without the Hercovici surname.

Go Sweep the Floor

With the profits from his stock, Grigore bought more properties. That was a valued investment at that time because renting apartments was easy, so no one could simply give up on their own. By the age of 25 – even without much planning – Grigore was a rich man. He possessed shares along with 12 properties: three stores and nine apartments. He lived in Leme with his mother and received income from all the other properties. He no longer depended upon working at the wrecking company for income, so he quit.

His purpose was to enjoy life. His role model, Uncle Leopoldo, lived as a carioca playboy: single, with money and no need to work. Grigore had achieved success and a lot was still ahead.

The only thing he could not predict was the fact that it was hard to enjoy life. He got bored easily. This initial feeling got worse and worse, and in a short time, Grigore walked along the beach feeling very confused and apathetic with a huge void. An anguish that would not let go of him. These were all symptoms that led to an existential crisis.

He was a rich man with a poor affective life. He did not manage to attract the women he wanted, least a woman to share his feelings, joys and sadness. In summary, he lacked a girlfriend with whom he could talk and confide.

On the contrary, affective bonding for him was similar to a sad and foggy afternoon. His mother was slipping deeper into her depression, and Grigore saw himself more and more a hostage of this unhealthy attachment she nourished with him. He was realizing that she was the solid obstacle between him and every having a healthy and loving relationship with a woman. Tonine did not spend a day without exposing her fears that one day her son would go off and get married, abandoning her, which would lead to her demise

Grigore was looking for a way out of this situation, any opportunity he could find. One day while walking down the street, he saw a poster for a lecture by a psychologist. He went into the lecture. The subject: a type of love, which was absorbing and directing the personality of the other. That was how he was feeling.

This symbiotic relationship with his mother would eventually produce worse things. He remembered the fatal words of the Romanian doctors, about the hereditary of her sickness. In the imagination of Grigore, his fate was the same. Like other members of his family, he had become successful; now, the next step was schizophrenia. He was afraid of the diagnoses, and thus he didn't go see a doctor. He preferred to take medicine on his own, which made him feel dizzy and distant from the world.

One day he went out in the street, feel dizzy and distant. He came across a lottery ticket seller. This man was missing an arm and most of his teeth, but he had a big smile. Grigore clearly remembers this meeting. He wished to be happy, moreover, to be the lottery ticket seller. That man had nothing but was happy; Grigore had everything but was deeply sad.

There were five consecutive years of emptiness and torment. It was the exterior emptiness due to the lack of activities, loving relations and the inner torment that would not leave him alone. He had a sedentary life with bad eating habits, which soon brought him illness. He was constantly sick, and only then, when he was 30 years old, did he start to look for doctors.

The first doctors were unable to detect a problem, much less propose a solution, which only increased the anguish. Grigore felt condemned to be sad. During an afternoon of despair, he rang the bell of a doctor who lived in the same building. He clearly expressed his wish: he wanted to be immediately admitted to the hospital, since he was afraid of doing something stupid. The darkness of the suicide of his aunt Lívia came out of the closet.

On this day, he managed to, in talking with the medical neighbor, calm himself. Nevertheless, he was far from a permanent solution. He then decided to seek out the most renowned – and more expensive – experts in the illnesses of the psyche in Rio de Janeiro. Doctor Donato Kulick still had the advantage of being Jewish, and who knows the affinity in the collective sufferings could help. It was not easy to schedule a consultation, but on the day Grigore was in the waiting room, he had enough antecedence and an enormous expectation. When the receptionist told him to enter, he was willing to open his soul.

And so he did. He reported to doctor Kulick, in the most truthful way possible, all the dramas and fears in his life, his existential emptiness. The doctor was listening with undivided attention. He had an attentive look and only made an occasional small nod. When Grigore finished his history, he waited. He was resigned to receive a prescription, internment, shocks even alternative treatments, he would accept anything.

The experienced doctor Kulick stood up to give more emphasis to the energetic tone of his diagnosis: "Go sweep the floor, kid!" He continued with a quite harsh sermon, the subject of which was for Grigore to stop being useless and go to work. Grigore was in shock with this unconventional method and with no anesthesia, Grigore only managed to ask the doctor before he left, what he thought he should do. "Anything", the doctor answered. "Get the first job you find."

Grigore left the doctor's office confused. However, it did not prevent him from following the doctor's advice to the letter. In the next building, there were several commercial establishments, and a job might be available there. One of the establishments had the suggestive name of "Golden Key". It was a realtor – a segment in which Grigore had experience – and, better. They were hiring. In that same moment, Grigore was working again, in accordance with the doctor Kulick's prescription.

And it worked.

Discovery of the World

Seven months later Grigore was the best broker in the company. He wasn't working for the money, because he didn't need it. His intentions were different. After realizing how much the lack of an activity was hurting his emotional stability, he dove into the work as if it were his salvation. He started to feel better, he dropped the self-medication and he wasn't anymore wandering the streets with sinister thoughts.

To conclude the sequence of positive changes only one thing in his life was missing. He needed a loving relationship. Being 30 years old, Grigore had one or two brief affairs, but nothing noteworthy. They were nothing even close to a true deep relationship. Love was a stranger.

Grigore also didn't do much to change that. His life was his work – and almost all brokers were men – caring for his mother and the constant visits he had with his uncle Leopoldo. He soon met with destiny. When he least expected, while visiting his uncle, he met the woman of dreams.

Nadege Sebatião da Silveira – a name with origins from her Spanish and Portuguese grandfathers – was born in the state of Alagoas, in the city of Taquarana. More precisely at a place called Sítio Nicácia. It was a simple house, in the middle of a land site. Nadege and her three sisters grew up with no electric power or piped water. A place where the children were free to play free in nature.

When she was 13 years old, in 1969, Nadege followed the path of many northeastern Brazilians who were living hard times in their place of birth and decided to try their luck in Rio de Janeiro. She came with her maternal grandmother and an uncle seeking to find her father, who had migrated a few years before. Even after she found him, she preferred to live with a grandmother and two sisters who came before her. In the beginning, she felt absolutely terrified in this big city, but soon the need made her face her fears. At 15 years old, with little skills – she tended to a child at the plantation, this skill now had little value – she looked for a job. Considering that, she was use to domestic work from an early age, helping her mother and stepfather with tasks; she ended up finding work in homes that required nannies or housemaids. After going through a few of them, at 19 years old she started to work with uncle Leopoldo, as a housemaid.

Every day she saw the nephew of her boss, who worked nearby and was always around. He was different from Leopoldo, who lived in a huge apartment and had good clothes and expensive habits; the nephew seemed similar to her: a poor person. Grigore walked with torn shoes and worn-out clothes. In addition to not wasting money being vain, there was another reason Grigore tried to look poor. He feared that people – especially women, of course –got close to him because of his money. Regarding Nadege, because of his lamentable attire, he was not under this risk. The housemaid of uncle Leopoldo found it weird at first, but soon got use to the fact that the wealthy boss had a poor nephew.

The nephew suddenly started to look to her differently. In fact, she had noticed him first, more precisely, right away. "My heart beat changed", says Nadege. But she never had any kind of answer. Today, Grigore admits the experienced uncle Leopoldo noticed the interest of Nadege, and told his nephew, awakening the reciprocity she was expecting.

After the flirt phase, according to Grigore, they started a relationship, to know each other better and one afternoon on the rocks of Leme, he proposed to her. The synthetic narrative is justified not only because men in general are not so good at remembering details of a romance but, especially, because there are not many romantic moments along the path.

Nadege tells that the two of them stayed in the phase of glances for a long time. He was shy, and she completely unsociable. They never talked. Perhaps that was a love history destined to quickly die, if one day Grigore didn't let his intrepid side surface. It wasn't the best approach, that is a fact, but it was something. Then one day, when Grigore rang the bell and Nadege answered, he saw the opportunity. She said her boss had left, he told her he would wait. She went to the kitchen, to work. He waited a little in the living room, but soon he followed his heart. While Nadege was doing the dishes, Grigore grabbed her, mixing power with a dose of clumsiness. A little more subtle it would be certainly more appropriate, since the interest of Nadege was true. However, Grigore's method brought up all the fear of the great city monsters, and that time she could hear her mother and aunts in the state of Alagoas telling her saying to preserve her virginity, a task in which she had succeeded so far. His approach caused the instinctive fight of flight reaction. Since the fight with the nephew of the boss didn't go well, she chose the second option. Nadege tried to go out through the kitchen's door, but Grigore put his body in front of her, not knowing whether to continue his attempt to grab her or to try remedying things. The fact is that plan B also went wrong. Nadege was extremely thin, and the minimum gap Grigore had left between the door and his body became an escape route.

When the boss arrived, later, he was surprised that the housemaid was locked in her room, and not in school, to where she went every night. Since normally Nadege didn't cook dinner, Leopoldo let it be. She said nothing.

The housemaid's room became her shelter to where Nadege now went every time Grigore appeared. She was convinced that the nephew of the playboy boss only wanted to take advantage of her. In the living room, Grigore was convinced that he had made a great mistake, irretrievable.

Nadege decided for a radical measure: to look for another job. She couldn't focus on her work anymore with that situation. Boss Leopoldo found it weird, but didn't question that. When Grigore hear that, he once again felt relationships were not his strength.

Five months later, he received a phone call in his office. Surprise: it was Nadege on the line. She asked if he knew who was speaking. Of course Grigore did: he had been thinking about her for five months, bitter for being responsible for the end of a relationship that had not even started. However, Nadege seemed friendly. Her voice was not showing any intention of a late angry discussion on the kitchen episode. Grigore became confident and asked her for her phone number, promising to call.

For Nadege that sounded like the old seduction strategy. When she suggested that they meet, Grigore told her that he had to check his schedule. She already was fully convinced of what she wanted. In the previous months, she believed the new job would make her forget the previous one and everything that had occurred, especially Grigore. But her heart decided otherwise. She was in love, even if she was not feeding the feeling. In doubt, she kept on frequenting the neighborhood around Leopoldo's apartment. Who knows she might even have a casual meeting. She was buying things in the bakery where she knew Grigore went in the corner of the building, to try to simulate a walk by as soon as she could see him arriving. Unfortunately, in this whole time the meeting never happened.

One day Nadege returned to look for a coat she had forgotten in the apartment of the old boss. Her leaving was definitive, but an unconscious wish for an excuse to return. Leopoldo searched the entire apartment, even in the things of the new housemaid, but did not find such a coat. For Nadege, it was the weapon lacking. She got indignant, suspected that the coat could have been stolen by the new housemaid and threatened to claim her rights. After that, she proposed the exchange: she would not complain any more about the coat if Leopoldo gave to her his nephew's phone number.

A first, the former boss found it an absurd proposal, and questioned the fact of her wanting anything to do with Grigore. He argued that he was not giving his nephew's phone to anybody. The impasse was there. Then Leopoldo weighed in things: the nephew was big enough to know what he wanted, and he was avoiding a headache because of a lost coat. That was how Nadege got his work phone number.

As soon as she got into the street, she went to the first phone booth and called. Grigore played his game but a few days later he called her back, to the number of the new job she had gave him. They set a meeting. On the very first date, they asked one another if they had a boyfriend, partner, wife, fiancé or anything of the type. Both were satisfied with the negative answers that there was nobody in the way, such as an ex-fiancé, ex-boyfriend or ex-husband. They were new in love relationships.

They would discover everything about one another and like it very much. Grigore started to feel alive. He had the typical attitudes of those in love: he caught himself smiling all the time. He went to beach just to watch the sunset, he thought of her all day long. Nadege was also in a new world, new feelings, and the joy of living. It was the end of the sentimental desert and the start of the rainbow.

For Grigore it came so natural that one day, without any kind of special preparation, he invited her to live with him. Nadege was petrified initially – thinking perhaps she would be making another mistake, not this time. The shock was surprise and happiness: Nadege accepted right away.

Then came the doubt: to live where?

Grigore answered that he saw an apartment they could rent. In fact, it was one of his properties, but up to that time, Nadege had no idea that the beloved had such assets. Grigore insisted on preserving his poor farce. He wanted an assurance that she really liked him even without the money. He chose the most simple of properties: a one room near where he was living with his mother. The apartment where he lived, as a matter of fact he would never show Nadege, since it was too big for a guy wearing torn socks. The proposal was, therefore, that they should live in humbleness and face their difficulties together. If it worked out, they would marry. She accepted. Grigore took the plan so seriously that they spent a fair amount of time without furniture; and when they bought some, it was in poor condition. They were sleeping on the floor. Happy.

Night Tea

The drama at this time in his life was due to the depression of his mother contrasting with his happiness. The more time he spent with Nadege, discovering a new life, the more he found his mother at home giving up the will to live. Nina let nothing in between the lines: the fault for her sadness was the abandonment by her son.

A conflict that is hard to solve. The son always so attached now wished to flee, but accepted that it was causing the death of his mother. She would not let it rest. Every day she remembered that if Grigore got away it would be the final stage of her fragile health.

Walking between heaven and hell, Grigore continued with his relationship and invited Nadege to live with him. Nina knew that day would come. She tried to talk him out of it every way she could. She tried to convince her son that his humble girlfriend only wanted his money. That she was a Northern immigrant who had come looking for an opportunity and saw in him a pot of gold. It didn't work.

Not even the solemn statement she made before her son moved out, a gesture that would be the death of her.

During the time they were dating and sharing the same roof, the mother-in-law and the daughter-in-law were never formally introduced to each other. Nadege supported that situation as best she could, knowing that Nina hated her. Sometimes they crossed each other in the street – they were living nearby – but the mother of her future husband insisted in not knowing who she was.

Grigore was managing the best he could. He helped his mother as much as he could. Since Nina was already disconnected from assistance activities, Grigore was finding ways to keep her distracted. He financed a few trips his mother wanted, locally as well as abroad. Nina wanted to go to Israel to visit her relatives. Once there, she told him she would not be back, instructing her son to ship all her furniture. Grigore did it, always hiding it from her future wife. After all, a poor man could not handle expenses so high. Later his mother changed her mind and wanted to return to Brazil. Nina, the furniture and the relationship problems were back.

One day Nadege told Grigore she was pregnant. For the couple, this was a doubly unforgettable moment. Grigore had promised that if living together worked, they would get married. And it worked. In the harmony, in the happiness, in the difficulties and now with the arrival of the baby. Grigore proposed to Nadege.

There were still two rocks in the way. The first: Grigore had to reveal the farce he had lived all this time. He confessed he was rich and told the reasons why he lied. In addition, his worries about patrimony were still one of the primary concerns in his life. Therefore, he proposed a marriage in a separation property regime.

Nadege had no problem accepting that. She dated a guy who had nothing, shared a roof with a guy who had nothing – in the marriage she was expecting nothing.

The proposal would be much more difficult for whoever did it. Today, talking about his life, which was full of many hard times, it makes Grigore cry when he remembers his behavior. For his wife, it is water under the bridge. For Grigore, it is still an open wound, in spite of the hundreds time he said he was sorry. "The biggest fault in my life", he says. Along the years, he realized how much love his wife devoted to him, and how all his mistrust was absurd.

The second obstacle ended up being easier than he expected. After the pregnancy, the announcement of the marriage – and over time, what helps – Nina started to accept the son's relationship. She realized that her son was clearly happy. Finally the first meeting between Nadege and Nina occurred. A dinner prepared with great care and good doses of anxiety was the opportunity to receive the mother-in-law. Nina arrived, finally at her son's apartment she began to talk with her future daughter-in-law as if no conflict had ever kept them away. They seemed like old friends.

This was a very welcomed surprise. Soon they became real friends. The advice Grigore's mother would give to her later showed the dimension of that change.

Nina advised Grigore – more than just advice, a maternal order – that he should never divorce Nadege, who she considered a very special person. Nina not only accepted the marriage but she would be at the altar, as a bridesmaid.

Grigore saw himself in the best of both worlds. He felt he was starting a new family, with the three now meeting at their home, in his mother's home or going out to have dinner and talking about the new child they were expecting.

The contact was good to Nina. The schizophrenia was still cunning: without announcing, it brought paranoia outbreaks and panic attacks. At that time, the attacks were predictable; Nina spoke about conspiracies, people invading her house, neighbors conspiring to attack her. She insisted on the idea of exchanging apartments with her son, since hers was constantly watched and there was an evil plan to destroy her. She didn't even want a housemaid, since everyone who went there was compromised with the enemy. Medical follow-up was a constant need.

Grigore and Nadege first had their son, and then they got married. Grigore remembers the strong emotion of being a father for the first time, and the huge goof he made. Walking like the typical expectant father, back and forth in the door of the surgery room, Grigore felt tears when he heard the crying of a child. Moments later the nurse appeared with a baby in her arms. Grigore approached, cried, said that the child was beautiful and asked the nurse if he could hold it. Only then, the nurse was able to tell him she was taking the baby to its father, who was waiting in the next room. Resigned, Grigore waited for a new baby crying to allow him to do it all over again.

Nina seemed happy as a grandmother, though she felt out of place in this role. She hardly was alone with her grandson, but she liked to be near him. When she was not having dinner at the couple's house, she invited them to go out and experience the restaurants she had discovered in her wanderings throughout Rio de Janeiro. They went to restaurants in the neighborhood such as Alto da Boa Vista and even places little known and little attended. They were always sober and elegant, characteristics Nina admired.

During one Saturday night, Grigore received a phone call from his mother inviting him to something she liked. There went the three of them, as a family, to have tea in the Hotel Luxor penthouse, on Atlântica Avenue. Overlooking the sea of Copacabana, they talked about their favorite subject, little Gregório — who got the Portuguese version of the name of his father and, as a second name a tribute to his grandfather Emilian. Nina used to spend those nights very close to her son Grigore, but she also taught Nadege a thing she considered very important: etiquette. During each dinner, she taught details and postures to transform her daughter-in-law into a woman. During the night in Hotel Luxor, Nadege was passionately instructed to, under no circumstance, hold the teacup with the little finger raised, a sign of an unforgivable tackiness.

They had fun together. Nina was especially calm. It had already been a week since the crises stopped. She felt better. It was noticeable to Grigore and Nadege how well she was these last days. Grigore seldom had seen his mother that much at peace. Even with few friends, with whom she generally met to play cards, Nina had reached a reasonable level of emotional independence.

After the pleasant evening, Grigore left Nina at the door of her building and went home with his wife. In the middle of night, the police awakened him. His mother had jumped out of the 10th story window.

Afraid of Himself

During the long journey through insomnia that night — which ended when he slept to the sound of the voice of the Universal Church pastor, and who would trace a new course for his life — Grigore had his thoughts taken for everything that had happened until that time. The lack of sleep was taking Grigore to the past, to that time he felt the glory for the born of his son Gregório and the tragedy of his mother's suicide.

When he came to the building where his mother lived, her body was still covered lying on the ground. The distance, looking from the ground to the top of the building, was infinite. Now, in the bed of his apartment on the 10th floor, he was himself, eight years later, with the opposite perspective. Jumping off doesn't seem so distant.

With no sleep and tormented by his marriage crisis, his devils were taking over the room. His mother had spent the better part of her life with a disease chasing her, and her son felted an heir. "I was afraid of myself", Grigore says. That feeling was growing stronger each time he was in front of a window.

Grigore remembered how Nina entered into crisis with the death of her husband, but before that, she never spoke about it again. How she went ahead even with her paranoia showing her that there was always someone chasing her.

There are the memories of that absurd moment. On the night of the suicide, Grigore and Nadege left Nina at the door of her building, she said goodbye with a rare smile. Later, the police brought the news of her death. There was neither a note, nor an explanation. An accidental fall was highly unlikely. In addition to the family medical history and warnings from the doctors that it could happen at any time, her slippers were in front of the window – facing the window, side by side in careful arrangement – indicating that Nina carried out her planned intention calmly. The mother had managed to carry her emotional chains until she was 59 years old. Grigore was 35, and couldn't stand living anymore. The last of the series of tragic thoughts regarding his mother was always the same. In a narrative that directed Grigore to the most painful point, he was full of regret. Perhaps, if he had taken his mother to live with him and his wife. Perhaps if he had noticed a gesture or a sign during the night of their last tea. Perhaps if he could have read between the lines of Nina's soul that something bad was about to happen.

Perhaps it was time for him to carry out his fate.

Even the constant memories of Nadege that he had been an impeccable son, who took care of his mother all time, with daily visits without getting away the sentimental link, the weight of the death of his mother was immeasurably heavier than what he had felt when his father died. Though both were tragic circumstances, the affective bond with his mother had always been much deeper. His father was distant; Grigore and he did not talk much. With his mother, he felt guarded and protected. He eventually assumed the role as the person responsible for her. To bring her a little happiness, he bought the best apartment and paid for her trips. There was one time when she wanted to go to Buenos Aires. Two other times she went to Israel to be close to her family and to travel around Europe.

Nevertheless, with all that, Grigore thought, it did not change her fate. His illusion was that he could establish the course for his own life, which was collapsing.

To seek refuge in religion was something out of his principles. Occasionally he went to the synagogue on Barata Ribeiro Street to light a candle, not because he believed, but more for his friends who assured him that such a gesture might take his mother to the light she needed on the other side of life. His true faith was revealed in the talks he had with his wife, a devotee of Our Lady of Aparecida, or with a relative who wanted to take them to find relief in a Pentecostal church: the Bible is not the word of God, simply because God does not exist, he used to say, with disdain.

Therefore, one night, listening to Radio Copacabana, he was looking out the window. Looking to his side, he saw her wife sleeping and the abyss of anger, pain and grief that was separating them. They did not stop sharing the same bed, even with so many fights, but even that tie seemed so fragile. His tragedy was not only regarding his mother: love inside him was fading completely.

His thoughts during these sleepless nights were on love that fades away from the marriage. History was following the same itinerary of every night without sleep. A movie with a reverse script: from the happy beginning of the couple to that terribly sad end.

Grigore was trying to understand what had happened to him along the way.

CHAPTER 2 - Hell

Year of Grace

The year in which his mother killed herself, 1980, was actually one of the best in the life of Grigore. Married, with affective life finally stabilized, he also had the incomparable joy of having his first son.

In his professional life, everything was also well. After increasing his equity even more as a distinguished realtor, he resolved to start his own business. A shop at one of his properties, which was inside a shopping center in Copacabana, on Siqueira Campos street, closed for business. In its place, Grigore opened G.V. Administrator and Real Estate agency. With his initials, Grigore Valeriu had no problem becoming stable.

The difficulties he encountered were typical for everyday life. What Grigore could not imagine was that one of them would open a new door in his life.

His neighbor on the lower floor started to complain about a leak that was soaking into his bathroom. After many confrontations, the neighbor decided to sue. Grigore ordered an inspection to locate the concern, which proved he was right. The source of the leak was not his apartment, but a column in the building requiring repair.

Despite these findings, the uncompromising neighbor opted to proceed with the lawsuit. A cause virtually lost provided that in addition to having the inspection in his side, Grigore hired one of the big shots in legal practice in Rio de Janeiro, doctor Cesário, best man at his wedding.

Notwithstanding, on the day of the hearing Grigore was anxiously insisting that the lawyer should not forget to mention the inspection. Doctor Cesário was using all his experience to calm him, in the best "I got this" style.

During the hearing, this excess of confidence revealed to be a problem. As we see in sports, doctor Cesário thought the game was already won. While the rival attorney presented his evidence – using vocal inflections, drama and indignation about the terrible problem of the water leaking into the home and disturbing the life of his client – Grigore's lawyer talked little. The hearing concluded before his Grigore's strongest weapon, the inspection, was presented. The sentence: Grigore had to swallow the bitter taste of injustice. Even though he was not guilty and had evidence to prove it, he was forced to compensate the neighbor and to find a way to stop the leak.

The high cost provided a lesson: do not trust lawyers. If he was considered one of the best and performed poorly, imagine how the others would be. Since he was not willing to lose again, in case another problem arose, he decided: he would study Law and become an attorney. Thus, the blue-sky year was reaching its end with an important discovery in the life of Grigore. In Law, he found a vocation. In his very first year of college, he discovered that he loved the world of law. The fascination was a strong antidote against the tiredness of working hard during the day and studying during the night in the Brazilian Legal Sciences College. A study to which he was giving his best, so much that he concluded the course with twenty-five grades of an A. And because of that, during the 4th year in college, even considering he had not graduated yet, an administrative law professor called his best student to work with him in a federal authority.

There was one incident during Grigore's studies when he was in a class with the highest expert in Civil Law in Brazil at the time, Pompilio da Hora. From the top of his reputation and of his almost 6'4" height, plus his brilliant curriculum including studies in Italy, a victorious career and a humble origin, he was among the most respected teachers, as well as most feared. Pompilio did not allow his students to ask questions during the lectures. This rejection to questions, in addition to his stout profile and serious and strong voice made Grigore feel as though he was back in a Bucharest classroom. Those who had some authority — including professors — reproduced the style of the dictators. The classroom was a microcosm of the country.

Grigore was not in Romania anymore, and his personality was quite different. Now, he was not willing to swallow information or an idea that made no sense. He was used to deeply investigating his subjects of interest, comprising several points of view and comparing several opinions. In summary: he learned to question.

The chance to face this dictator came a day in which Pompilio was talking about usable and unusable goods. In law, that is the differentiation between ordinary goods, which are replaceable, and special goods, which are unique and cannot be found anywhere else. For the replaceable ones, Pompilio used the example of a horse.

It was then that a brazen hand was lifted in the middle of the class, under the frightened stare of the other students. Even if the reason was to ask to go to the bathroom it would be audacious, disrespectful to the status of the renowned professor. But it was worse: it was for a disagreement. Grigore argued that there were special horses, which could not be compared with none other and neither replaced. And as proof, he looked for a real example. At that time, the sport magazines were praising a non-human hero: the horse Aporé, which during the Brazil cup had just won the Triple Crown that year in Brazilian horse racing.

Grigore concluded his insubordinate act believing he had a solid argumentation that could hardly be disregarded. The counterblow was very different from everything he had seen in legal debates. "You, kid, do you know what a horse is?" asked the teacher in his loudest voice. "A Horse is that animal with four hoofs, mane, tail..." And he gave the full description of the animal as if the listener had not idea of what it was.

From that point on, Grigore was singled out. To be accepted, he needed an average grade of a 7. Pompilio almost gave the taste of victory to his insolent student. In the two exams, he gave a 6 and a 7, having corrected them with further great severity. Therefore, on the final exam – already a little more casual and possibly appreciating the clash – Pompilio commented to the students that they had a person in there that should be present. Grigore required the highest grade to be established as the best student. Not a 10, but the highest grade professor Pompilio da Hora used to give to his students – an 8.

He did it. He got an 8 and began to win the respect of the master. The following year, they started to talk more, discussing law and legal matters, especially in the area that would become the greatest passion for Grigore for the rest of his life, Civil law. This was the subject that he would end up teaching as a professor years later.

On that semester exam, Grigore did get the grade 10, which was the first ever given by Pompilio da Hora in all his years of teaching.

This was still just the beginning of Grigore's recognition of the strong ties which started to join them. Once, during a walk around the campus, Pompilio dropped his defenses before Grigore. He talked about his history, as the son of a housemaid adopted by her bosses, who spent his whole life trying to prove his value. One of the hardest battles he encountered was when he took the exam to be a judge. During the oral assessment, he presented to the assessment body all his virtues, the results of an effort high above the average of any student. He made a faultless presentation. And he failed.

Nobody in the examining body managed to provide a convincing explanation as to why he failed. Grigore was also curious during this conversation and wanted to know why a man this brilliant had not managed to become a judge at last. Pompilio stretched out his arms to Grigore, showing his black skin.

Grigore started to act as his own attorney, as he had predicted. In the real state agency, there were plenty of contracts to be adjusted.

Brilliant lawyer and successful businessman, Grigore describes his personality in those years of glory. "I stomped over corpses to get things." As a realtor, he remembers, he had the guts his bosses loved and he was hated by his colleagues. To get distinction, he didn't care who he crossed.

As a boss in his real state agency, he was strict and insensible. Grigore was living that phase where he felt like he owned of world. He played a character that would not allow anyone to get close. He would not accept being called by his name. He insisted that he be called "Doctor". His status and diplomas gave him knowledge and arrogance. He neither smoke nor drank but today he admits his addiction was to "despise".

From the Desert to the Harem

Such personality traits were not limited to his professional life. The desert which had been his love life and the contact with women during his adolescence could now become an oasis. The conditions were given: if before he faced repression by communist Romania, he was displaced to a new life in another country and the proximity with the sick mother. Now he was feeling a part and player of Rio de Janeiro by the sea. It had the sun, healthy lifestyle and mainly, beautiful women. On the plus side, he was young, rich, a sportsman and looked like a father which was compared to nobody less than Frank Sinatra.

The foggy times of the past had been left behind. All these elements made him notice that his interest in women was reaching a new high level. The arrogance had as its side effect, the inflated ego of one whom is capable of everything. "I considered myself the guy", says Grigore.

Everything was going a way to make him compensate for the years without a companion. On the other hand, a huge detail: the marriage, which was going well.

With his wife, he attended college dinners and every weekend they went to the beach, where they were part of a pioneer group. Grigore, his wife and his friends were among the first ones to practice a sport that today is common in Rio de Janeiro beach and became an Olympic sport: beach volleyball. Together they got wood to bury in the sand to set the net, they arranged the ball, the field lines and, with a full planning, they also built one of the first showers pumping seawater in the sand near the sidewalk – this would soon become common, but at that time it was rare. They also got a license, which was not easy. Only then, with everything ready, could they practice their hobby - almost an addiction, since every weekend they were playing – on the sands of Copacabana, having as neighbors a group that preferred soccer and which included the experts Jairzinho and Telê Santana.

In all those places – beach, college, work, neighborhood – Grigore dealt with the opportunities for relationships with other women and resisted. For seven years, Grigore followed the good guy manual. But we can't say the same for the following two years.

The clandestine lifestyle of a married man with regular affairs became his life. In all cases, he followed a similar script: the affairs never lasted long; he warned since the start that he would not divorced Nadege and he was always felt brutally guilty. "I felt like a scoundrel each time my wife caressed me", says Grigore.

The dates were always in the afternoon, provided at night he was a family man. If he resisted for seven years, now his resistance was zero. He was not chasing any women, but he took any opportunity arising to him. Even if the women were much older or uglier than his wife was.

In most cases, his conflicts were only with the guilt and the intricate schemes he had to set in this clandestine lifestyle especially when his wife knew his lover, which happened on several occasions. With the first one, she was a colleague in college, with which Nadege would sometimes fraternize. "What hurt me more was to know that everyone else knew what was going on but me", says Nadege.

The second one was more complicated. Grigore had an affair with the upper floor neighbor – today affectionately nicknamed by Nadege as "the witch of 72" – and he thought that his method of making clear his intentions of not getting serious would work. He was deeply wrong. More than out of spite, this nickname was given for a reason. The neighbor attended macumba meetings, an African religious practice similar to voodoo, and she did not like to be in the role of a fleeting lover, although she also was married.

The harassment began with insinuations and veiled threats. Soon the "witch of 72" began to appear in common places, such as the beach, and to spread malicious gossip about the couple Grigore and Nadege, teasing with the nicknames they had for each other: sweetheart and dear.

Things got really serious the day Grigore arrived for his volleyball match at sunset – an opportunity to ease the mid oppressed by guilt – and next to the bar supporting the net he saw a dead chicken, a bottle of rum and a candle. This was a traditional spell of the macumba. Skeptic and angry, he did not think twice: he kicked everything and announced that the match would start. But the game did not reach its end. Grigore had to stop with strong pains in his arm and had a hard time breathing. Coincidence or not, the latter was the same chronic problem the inconvenient lover had.

After two years and a few months, tired of his double, triple and sometimes quadruple life, Grigore decided to tell everything. He thought it would ease his conscience, which he considered a solution. This was yet another mistake. If the confession amid the crying helped to calm the internal conflicts, now he had planted a long, deep and permanent conflict, which would leave him in a situation much worse than the previous one. Nadege could not accept this, neither on the day of the confession, when amid a nervous crisis she began to break objects in the house, nor many years later. These became the years during which the harmony of the couple was lost and replaced with an unstable balance, changing into fights, disillusion and dislike.

Fights and Tranquilizers

When the reality set in that the marriage collapsed in the mind of Nadege, she was waiting for their second son, Emiliano. Grigore confessed believing it would calm his inner nerves; now they both were in crisis.

Nadege was in shock. Her former calm and enthusiastic demeanor became reserved. She lost the smile. She couldn't accept the broken promises, the ones they made in the beginning of their relationship, to tell each other if one stops loving the other. There would never be infidelity.

The only way to go on was with the help of drugs. Now she was the one living in physicians' waiting room. The difference regarding her husband's crisis some years before was that her anguish had a clear reason. Nadege had always thought she was the only one. She completed him. Her pink and flowery marriage turned grey and wilted. The times of fights and conflicts surpassed the times of calmness. Everywhere they went, she thought Grigore was flirting with other women. Mistrust overpowered her imagination, and she starting to be sure her husband was setting meetings behind her back. Such paranoia was making her see conspiracies of women allied to her husband to deceive her. She had fits of jealous rage, in public and at home. A pretty woman on the television was enough for an endless fight, when they relived their sorrows. A discussion in the car while they drove was enough to make her open the door and threaten to jump out.

Divorce was close. Nadege packed and got out of their home with the children, but she only managed to get to the sidewalk. Behind her, her husband pleaded for her to come back.

Conversations were more like interrogations. Nadege called her sister in Juiz de Fora daily. She asked for advice, but what she wanted more was to understand how she could keep loving and hating at the same time.

From doctor to doctor, with a diagnosis of depression, she ended up with the same doctor Donato Kulick, who had taken Grigore out of his abyss and got him to work. Grigore was optimistic of finding a miraculous cure for Nadege and rescuing their marriage in the process. They went there together, but the heterodox doctor Kulick left Grigore in the waiting room: he needed to talk with his wife alone.

In the doctor's office, the discussion was not about Nadege getting a job. Lighting a cigarette in in one hand, doctor Kulick defended his position that there was no need for any special treatment, only that Nadege needed to understand that men really were that way. If she understood that, everything would be easier.

From the waiting room, Grigore saw his wife leaving in a flurry of emotions, amid curses; she told the doctor he was the one that needed treatment. Her own diagnosis was that her husband was a sick man.

Considering that doctor had helped Grigore and his mother, Nadege agreed to come back to another appointment much calmer, but with her suspicious temperament even more sharp. Cautious, doctor Kulick opted for more traditional methods. Nadege does not remember the name of the imported medicines to control the lithium dosage in the blood she was taking that time. Only that they were large pills, which did not pass easily through her throat, and so hard that they only dissolved in water with great effort. These medicines were causing side effects such as lethargy and the sensation of being constantly drugged. "Our life was all about fights and tranquilizers", Nadege exclaimed.

When negotiating was possible, the couple tried to find ways to get through the past and forge ahead to the future. Grigore ended up closing his real estate agency, and in the same place he opened a clothing shop – sales were on the bottom floor and the office was on the mezzanine. He believed a change in routine could help him. Additionally, he called Nadege to work with him; however, there was little work. The real reason, and they both knew it, was to keep Nadege near her husband all day, in an attempt to ease her chronic mistrust. Now they were spending 24 hours a day together, most of which was arguing.

They tried a change of environment. They left the apartment where they were living, filled with bad memories, and went to a house with a swimming pool in the neighborhood of Barra da Tijuca. This did not work and became yet another drama added to their family issues. Six months later, afraid of robberies, they decided to move into another apartment, this one on the 10th floor, still located in Barra da Tijuca.

They next attempted a spiritual solution to their problems, one by unorthodox means. The daughter of Nadege's stepfather indicated a pai-de-santo - an African cult priest - who was known for solving absolutely everything. The problem was that the wonder-worker lived in São Paulo. Even so, Grigore and Nadege went there. It was not a simple consultation. During the first set of sessions, the couple had to attend, for several hours, in the house of the priest, for a three-day period. Each day a blessing, followed by a prayer in which the priest invoked God to embody them, to bless the couple.

Saving the marriage demanded an endless number of prayers and rituals. They started to live in a world of symbolism, where the life of the couple was in a dusty bottle in a room in the priest's house.

The voodoo phase would bring some extra hitches. Even when they were in Rio de Janeiro, they were required to follow the proposed rituals. A dagger shall be driven into a list containing the names of our enemies. It could not be any ordinary kitchen knife; it had to be a dagger. It shall strike the list at a specific time of a specific day, the precise time the priest in São Paulo would be performing a prayer. The synchronicity of times would require perfectly adjusted clocks and a careful effort. During the evening, we had to light candles inside shoes boxes and the following day we had to report to the priest what drawings the candle wax had formed. A difficult description, especially by telephone and considering that the forms had no geometrical criteria at all.

Grigore and Nadege regularly travelled for new consultations. After a while, they realized that in truth they got in trouble. In addition to the unproductive results, during their visits, they ended up realizing that the man who was promising peace walked with a bushwhacker in his waist, had problems with his neighbors and was always getting into fights. Worse, they saw some voodoo that the priest did with the intention of killing enemies.

It was during one of those trips to São Paulo that they decided to stop in the city of Aparecida do Norte. Nadege was a devout of Santa Aparecida, and the frame of the famous cathedral they saw from highway Dutra seemed like an exit for the pains of the soul. The convinced atheistic Grigore agreed to take home a plaster bust with the image of Jesus Christ. He was still not a believer, but in the middle of the night, not being able to sleep, he crossed the corridor separating the bedrooms from the living room and stopped in front of the statue. Before Christ, he made a sort of reverse Pascal's wager[*]. He talked to Jesus and said with honesty that he did not believe in him. However, he thought, if he existed and truly had all that power people said he had, he should help him to get out his situation. This was a strange negotiation, which served at least to let him vent. It was not the first time he cried before the sculpture, thinking on his small children who were suffering with the discord of the parents and feeling the deep suffering which seemed endless.

It was during one of those nights that the messages of Radio Copacabana got to his ears. In the first night, Grigore slept, and woke up the next day restored. The following nights, the phenomenon was repeated. Grigore had tried several tranquilizers, but none seemed better than the hypnotic voice of the pastor. In the third night, he invited Nadege to hear Copacabana with him, and both of them did not get past the first twenty minutes of the sermon. They slept like babies, more and more intrigued by their new discovery.

On one of the nights, making an effort to pay attention, Grigore and Nadege heard the pastor say that listening to the word of the Lord on the radio was good, but not good enough. There was a call to the radio regulars to attend services, to know the truth up close. If God's voice had changed the life of the listener, the pastor was arguing, imagine what would happen when they find Him in full.

Sheep Full of Wool

The brand new Belina Ghia model car contrasted with the simplicity of the place. The others few vehicles at the temple doors were old bicycles. It was not exactly a temple, since the name suggests an imposing building. On the contrary, the Universal Church of the neighborhood of Recreio dos Bandeirantes, western side of Rio de Janeiro, was a brick shed such as so many others in the slums surrounding it. It was 1988, and the only temples of the Universal Church that had the luxury of upholstered seats were the in Botafogo, on Clement Street, and in Abolição, on Suburbana Avenue.

In Recreio dos Bandeirantes, the chairs were made of rotten wood and the ground was cement. Grigore and his wife sat and waited for the service, listed as a half hour service on a paper scribbled in the wall.

This was enough time, Grigore thought, for this new feeling to take over him. Faith, absent in his education in communist Romania, was a feeling that was before fully rejected, now started to plant its seeds. After the night in which the sounds of Radio Copacabana made him sleep and forget the idea of suicide, the

---

*Blaise Pascal, a XVII century philosopher, argued that the belief in God was a wager. The rational thinking in fact had no reason to believe in God: He could exist or not. Therefore, the man had to make the most convenient choice. In this case, if the man bets God exists and, in fact, He exists, the prize of the wager is high. On the other side, if the bet is for atheism and the gambler is right, he does not lose anything, since never believed anyway. So, Pascal demonstrates, it is a better deal to bet on God's existence.

war with his wife was now a truce. Both started to hear the voice of the pastor every night. They lacked peace. The faith brought together a still vague but mighty feeling that life would work out.

In that first service, the sedative effect was stronger. And that, instead of meaning lack of interest, was everything they wanted. The workers - pastor assistants in charge of solving daily issues and keeping the temple working — upon the end of the service approached them to get to know the couple better. In the following week, Pastor Geraldo himself gave special attention to the new worshipers. Today, Nadege understands the siege with clarity: "As soon as they saw us, they thought: sheep full of wool have arrived".

The Universal Church structure was incipient, but already had their goals established. The pastor submitting the best collections was the one to move up in hierarchy. The more the worshipers were generous the more the temple gets points with the higher administration. Grigore and Nadege were in that poor environment a gift from heaven.

The first donations were discreet amounts of cash placed in the little church bag. Then, during the service, urged by the pastor to free them from their attachment. Valuables were placed upon an open Bible. Most of them had emotional value, for the sacred book nearly always received trinkets and things bought from street vendors. Soon pastor Geraldo sermons convinced Grigore that he could not be a cheapskate before God. At last, if someone there could make a difference on behalf of such important work it was him. One day, moved after a sermon on the generosity before God, Grigore left over the Bible a watch he liked very much that had not only emotional, but also material value.

The pastor became closer to his new sheep. From this friendship, he earned not only rides from his far away house in Campo Grande, but also donations for the church such as a fridge, a radio, a TV set. Grigore and Nadege were proud to contribute. Faith started to yield fruits. Grigore finally decided to open the Bible and study the Gospels and the life of Jesus. Like everything he did, he went deep into it, and the spirit transcendence feeling invaded him. The life of the couple was improving. The arguing was more scattered and lighter. Grigore was becoming calmer. His hard breathing, a problem since his childhood, was showing signs of improvement. He got to the point of being able to stop using tranquilizers, which had been an inseparable companion.

There was nothing greater in life than rewarding the man and place providing those blessings to him. Recreio dos Bandeirantes is a neighborhood known for having everything very far from the houses. To go to the bakery or to the supermarket, for example, you would need a car. Grigore and Nadege were the few ones in their new community that didn't need to do everything on foot. Thus, it would not hurt to buy milk and food and deliver it at the house of the pastor Geraldo in Campo Grande, would it? What was the cost of the donations, for they had money but could not buy peace?

Additionally, they felt important. For the pastor Geraldo, Grigore and Nadege had a divine mission. The couple started to admire more and more that man for his faith. For Pastor Geraldo, everything was possible to get for God's work. He used to say that if one day he did not get anything: "I'll close the church and I'll tear up the Bible". In actuality, he got everything, especially with the valuable support of his new sheep.

The Devil's Finger

As soon he won the trust of his new sheep, Pastor Geraldo started his first gospel mission: to destroy the house of the couple.

Grigore and Nadege were honored by the pastor's first visit to their home. After all, they had a man of God in their home. They received him with smiles that contrasted the seriousness with which the pastor was looking at the environment. His eyes ran through the pictures on the walls, the china, the chandelier, the furniture, and he seemed to not like what he was seeing.

More and more embarrassed, Grigore asked if there was something wrong. Pastor Geraldo was incisive: this house was taken over by objects owned by the devil. The man of God started to point, furiously, the corruption in each statue expressing Greek art, the baroque angels representing the decadence of the Catholic Church that worshipped images, the sensuality of the Renascence artists. The house that for the couple was always in good taste was now a den of depravity and decadence. The drawings made with great care in the tea cups, with portraits of the family had to be removed in the name of detachment. A pot with the image of a sheep that seemed to carry the horn of the devil, a porcelain coach with the image of Saint George, the feminine images in the pictures on the walls, each detail of the decorations, of the china, each painting. Was the pomba-gira, an African cult entity, or the devil who, insidious, was invading the life of the couple?

Grigore and Nadege got frightened when the pastor threw a plate against the wall. Before their astonishment, Pastor Geraldo got a broken piece from the ground and showed the drawing that remembered Venus de Milo: sensual and without the arms, the image of doom itself.

And thus, abruptly, the visitor started to throw plates, cups, chinaware, decorations against the walls. He tore pictures, knocked down statues. Grigore and Nadege just watched the holy wrath in a mixture of surprise and wonder. Especially when they saw the pastor approach, the sacred image of Christ in the corridor and abruptly, threw it in the ground and kicked the broken pieces with anger. A domestic version of which some year's later Bishop Von Helder would do on TV, kicking the statue of a saint and outraging Catholics throughout the country.

The pastor only stopped after showing signs of fatigue. On the ground and on the walls, the destruction indicated the defeat of the devil. There was much work to be done, but the pastor comforted us telling us he would return.

And he did. During the following days pastor Geraldo returned, regularly, to break what needed to be broken. The couple not only got used to that, but they were certain that this was the reason why their marriage faced serious issues: the eyes of the devil watched them all around, and even inside their own house.

The pastor assured them that his actions would free the couple from the strings binding them to the past. In addition to the destruction, other methods were required to erase the old dramas. The family pictures, the marriage pictures, the register of Grigore and Nadege love history and, especially, the pictures with Grigore's mother. These were all eliminated in a bonfire. After a while, the couple started to believe in that passage rite. Though they only had just the sofa in home their faith was growing strong.

In the center of the large dining table, Pastor Geraldo found the most pernicious object. A heavy porcelain coach, almost one meter long. The passengers were images of half-naked women and, worse, Romans carrying swords. Yes, Romans who symbolized the apostolic Roman church. The sinners met in that coach.

Therefore, the pastor warned us that the object would be broken during the service, so that all worshipers could witness the victory of the powers of Good. The couple, Grigore and Nadege, would then be fully freed from the evil surrounding them.

During service the following day, before the attentive eyes of the audience, the pastor boasted his deeds at the home of the new worshipers and showed the Satanic object. With the coach in his hands and imbued with hatred and courage, he cursed against the lewd women and the Romans. He preached, screaming that the object was made with the hand of the devil and threw it hard to the ground.

During the ordeal, his finger was caught in one of the many projections of the coach. The weight of the object cut off the finger. In shock, Pastor Geraldo saw his finger cut off, but still attached to the hand by the joints. The following scene was the first disappointment of Grigore and Nadege with the men of the Universal Church. The person, who called himself a man of God, always determined and brave for being protected by the Lord, now was crying in despair for the cut off finger. The man who challenged the devil was now a frightened lamb. In the hospital – to where Grigore and Nadege took him in their car – the pastor was shaking, and alternated sorrows with uncurbed crying that made the environment uncomfortable. It was lucky that the owners of the car were careful to wrap the finger, hoping something could be done.

In fact, the pastor had his finger reattached. He started to proudly show off the work performed by God. O his hand, the finger was almost as perfect as it was before. On his wrist, the prized watch Grigore donated to the church.

Collective Myopia

Upon entry into the Universal Church of the Kingdom of God made Grigore a new man. It does not mean he changed for better. His attendance at the church started to become intense, most of time during three daily services, in addition to the time spent with the pastor. Grigore felt faith changing his life. If he once carried traumas because of the deaths of his parents, if he once had an emotional life full of scars, if he had sinned and felt the weight of guilt, now he was able to do unbelievable things. He tells of a particular time when he was walking near the Central do Brazil train station. He came across a striking movement not friendly at all. The uproar was intense. There was a risk of trouble and of people getting hurt. Grigore considered going back, but as a faithful man believing in his strength, he decided to continue ahead. Then the crowd of strikers opened while he passed such as the sea had opened for Moses.

His wife, on the other hand, was nowhere near as close as his involvement with the faith, and with the church. Nadege early on started to sense a bad smell in the air, in the insistent requests for donations, in the behavior of the pastors and their wives, which most times were not in accordance with what they preached. She had abandoned her jewels, rings, earrings and bracelets in agreement with the words of a pastor called Randal, who like many others assured vanity was a weapon of the devil. The women needed only to bath, nothing more. However, in the church Nadege was seeing the pastor's wife wearing a leather coat and contact lenses of different colors each day – always in a way to match the color of the clothes.

Another strange thing happened in a ceremony called the Last Supper, performed by the Universal Church once every month. A noble ritual, in which the pastors mirrored Christ's gesture of distributing the bread and the wine: a way to honor the alliance with God. Such as in the original Last Supper, the worshipers fed frugally. Nadege was surprised when one night during the ritual she went to the second floor of the temple and saw the colored contact lens bimbo with her children having their own private supper. Different from the solemn tone happening on the lower floor, good manners lacked there. The supper had nothing to do with being sacred: the boys, encouraged by the mother, were eating the bread as if they were starving; the mother hardly finished swallowing and already washed the wine down her throat.

The abyss between speech and act by the leaders of the Universal Church was gross. Nadege remembers especially a philanthropic event in which she was involved. The needy were people from her home state, Alagoas, who were in a precarious situation because of a flood that destroyed the city of Maceió. Worshipers mobilized and donated coats, food, and any type of assistance. On the other hand, the Universal Church promoted the assistance without donating anything. Even the trucks transporting the provisions were sponsored by the members. The resources the church received in donations were never used to help the neighbor. On the contrary, sometimes – and Nadege saw – when the Universal Church received large amounts of food to give to those who were hungry, a good part did not reach their destination. Inside the temple, workers and pastors separated the better quality food for the temple meals. The rest were for the needy.

Grigore also witnessed a good part of such ominous behavior. While the pastors censured worshipers who contracted debts, Grigore saw some of them sunk in worries because of nonpaid installments. While they condemned the use of medicines, since that meant the worshiper did not trust the power of God, the pastors were always seeing the better doctors and using medicine.

The difference is Grigore witnessed all that but refused to see. Nadege knew her husband had found the Universal Church in a sensible state. But now he was a fanatic.

Their dedication and involvement with church, which had been the remedy for their conjugal fights, was now causing them. Nadege knew her husband was becoming increasingly blind to the contradictions of the Universal Church.

Blindness had led him to wish to be cured only by faith of the 7-diopter myopia he had since he was a child. In the first great mass service the Universal promoted, in Maracanã stadium – and occurred every year showing the new power in the kingdom of faith – Bishop Edir Macedo told everyone with glasses, among the more than 100 thousand worshipers attending, to throw them away.

The lawn and the seats of the stadium who 40 years before were the theater of biggest collective crying of that nation – the defeat of the Brazilian team in the final of 1950 Soccer World Cup – was now the stage of an attempt of a collective miracle. Glasses of different forms were thrown on the lawn and on the ground of the seats. Short-sighted, astigmatic and far-sighted persons threw away their glasses with faith and fury, trusting the voice of Bishop Macedo, who assured they would see in the following moment.

Grigore was one of them. His wife found it weird, clearly, but how could she be heard amidst such a collective purification? Grigore prayed, raised his hands to the heavens, and cried out, as most of them did, but he couldn't see things in focus. Now he only could follow the sermon by hearing: he could not distinguish at a distance the man of God who had convinced him he would see. No one realized that, on the stage, Bishop Macedo and a few followers such as pastor Renato Suhuet had their glasses on during the remainder of the sermon. For both of them, whom Grigore would later find out, were cured of their myopia by the true miracle of laser surgery.

The speech, however, was different. Bishop Macedo now was telling those who could not see that they didn't have enough faith, since they still hadn't accepted God in their hearts. This revealed one of the most common and effective *modus operandis* of the Universal Church: if things were getting better for the worshiper, the merit was to God and to the church, which acts as an intermediary; if they did not improve, the worshiper was blamed for being not ready yet.

On that day, Grigore only had eyes for his conversion. He returned home shortsighted visually, as well as spiritually. He was clueless to see the hoax he got himself into or the road ahead of him taking them back to Barra da Tijuca. Grigore risked driving with 7-diopter myopia, believing he would be gifted with perfect vision eventually. His wife, in the passengers' seat, was convinced that would not happen. It was one more of many fights they had because of the Universal Church, which only ended when the car went off the road and ended up in a brush field. A year later Grigore had no car – sold for a price under market value to speed his donation to the church –, his wife was having to make collect calls from a phone booth to her sister in Juiz de Fora to complain about her life – since the telephone was cut – and the fights were getting worse.

Not even with history from his son Emiliano, who told him of the time of the Maracanã service that year would make Grigore change his mind. The boy had become friends with the son of one of the lead pastors of the Universal Church. During worship services, the two friends were playing in one of the internal rooms of Maracanã stadium, while they saw bags and bags of money. Emiliano asked his father to stay with his friend after the service. With the authorization of Grigore, Emiliano left in one of the many cars of the convoy of pastors for a mansion with a swimming pool in the city of Niterói. There, little Emiliano saw inside the Universal Church's spree. While the pastors were enjoying themselves in the swimming pool, happy with the majestic result of one more mega event, a retinue of workers separated and counted the money arriving in the bags, with the care to straighten out each bill brought from the pockets of the worshipers.

Going back home, Emiliano reported this and received a response from Grigore that the pastors deserved the prosperity. The son was ok with that. What he did not understand was why the pastors' children spent the afternoon playing video game when months before his father had sold his saying that he heard in church that video games were entertainment from the devil.

Grigore, as always, looked for answers where he expected to get them, with the pastors. They had to know the way; after all, they were God's emissaries. Then he was shocked to hear from pastor Oswaldo, who was ministering the worships in Recreio dos Bandeirantes at the time, that Nadege was possessed by the devil. The strong personality of the wife – typical of her home state of Alagoas – was, according to the church, the presence of the evil one. Grigore had already seen and heard often in the services mentions to the devil, Satan, dust devil, mud devil, maria padilha, zé pilintra and so many others names by which evil was known, and how the devil dominates the body, the mind and heart of the weak. Now the evil was over his wife. Although she was completely dedicated to the church, this made no sense at all.

Even so, during a rough night of arguing, Grigore held both arms of his wife firmly, as the pastors used to do during exorcism rituals, and began to shout telling the devil to leave Nadege's body. She was outraged by the improvised exorcism of which she was being a victim, and that only increased her anger. The result was very different from what Grigore used to see in the services, when the pastor always defeated the devil and the worshiper stayed in peace. At home, Grigore had no means to eradicate the devil, as it seemed to happen in church, and the discussion became more heated.

During one of their many fights, it was common to see Nadege break plates, cups and anything she saw in front of her during fury outbursts. Different from the destruction promoted by pastor Geraldo years before, the goal now was not to expel the devil, but to expel the church itself from the life of the couple. Nadege was convinced that they were being deceived, and hated to see that her husband could not realize this. Worse yet, he was defending the pastor, not her.

During a raining day, when Grigore left walking through the mud to walk the seven kilometers to the temple, Nadege threatened not to be there when he returned. Grigore went ahead: the Lord's word above all things. But he was between the devil and the deep blue sea. If on one hand divorce was everything the pastor wanted – and advices in this direction were increasingly incisive – on the other hand to preserve the marriage was a matter of honor. Divorce was a moral fault, a defeat. Especially after having sworn before his mother during her last days that he would never divorce Nadege, after go through everything they had gone through.

Grigore returned home and saw that his wife did not keep her promise. She did not go away, but she also never returned to the Universal Church. From there on, Church was definitively between them.

The Power of Faith

If there is one thing you cannot hold against the Universal Church it is that they lack creativity. If the goal was to collect money, the means of convincing the worshipers to contribute were greatly seductive and diversified.

The efficacy of the method depended on the skill of the pastor in combining the ingredients: guilt, constraint and the blind faith of the worshiper. On the other hand, the pastor's profile required him to have no constraint. Maximum ambition above all. "A shy pastor pitying the sheep is not good enough", explains Nadege.

Pastor Geraldo, of Recreio church, for example, was clever in creating sermons with a happy conclusion, which insured generous donations. Sometimes during worship services he laid down on the unfinished cement ground and told the worshipers he would not stand up until we got 5,000 cruzados novos – around $ 3.000,00 USD – for God's work. The challenge surprised those in attendance, after all considering all of the families there; it was possible to get that amount. The pastor insisted that the money would appear. He knew that he would not be going to lie on his back on the cold hard cement for much longer: Grigore and Nadege started to attend the services with more frequency, and that would be the first opportunity to test how generous they would be in the name of faith. The money, for which pastor Geraldo was praying to God for, with eyes facing the ceiling of the church, was there, a couple of feet from him, in the checkbook Grigore carried in his pocket.

Before that performance, there was no way to wait much longer. There was, after all, the constraint, since all the worshipers were praying with hope and knew that the man who would make the pastor stand up was among them. The hints sent by the pastor in his prayer were becoming clearer and clearer. He even said that he was feeling that one of the new worshipers out there had a "ruffian in the heart", a slang to say that the worshiper was attached to material things. And that was God speaking.

Grigore did not doubt that. Pastors were the secretaries of God and thus unchallengeable. So he went to the pulpit and proudly left on the table in front of the altar a check in the amount requested. The pastor promptly got up, giving graces and amens to God. All the church prayed louder in the climax of consecration. The commemoration was becoming a collective purification, since the strength of the pastor was validated. It was not the man Grigore who solved the money problem, but the faith of the pastor who heard God's call telling him what was going to happen. That is one of the great skills of the men in Universal: to capitalize for themselves upon someone else's actions. Pastor Geraldo got the three thousand dollars and more admiration from his flock.

The monetary request did not stop when this goal was reached, since it was way beyond this amount. Taking advantage of the symbolic gesture of unselfishness and the emotional environment he created, pastor Geraldo called for a collective detachment. He told the worshipers to undress their vanity and turn over their earrings, rings, bracelets. They needed money for the bus, for snacks for their children, the pastor called everyone to turn their pockets inside out to prove to God the power of their love.

This is the most effective argument in the temples of the Universal Church. Who is not giving does not love God. It is cruel, simple and efficient. If the worshiper decides to give, then he gives it all. After all, as the pastors argue, if you really love you do not give a bad gift. On the contrary, you give everything you have, the best you got. There were even the worshipers with only a small amount of change in their pockets at months end. They were told that they should give it all as to not insult God. It would confirm their unselfish and complete love. Those who had three thousand dollars, such as Grigore, should leave that amount in the collection basket. Those who had their last money of the month should give it away for the cause. Those who had just the money for their medicine, stop taking it. To stress this point, in case somebody did not understand the message, the pastors would speak about punishments to those who are exposed and do not give to God: misfortunes, death of loved ones, a devastating cancer. The worshipers could choose what was better for them.

Medicines, vanity and installments are three critical points in the Universal Church's speech. Those three points are emphasized intensely. Why do you need medicine if God is going to heal you? Does the worshiper by chance not believe in the power of the Lord? Vanity was attachment to the material world, at best, and the worst kind of communion with the devil. To find God people do not need earrings, watches, make-up, necklaces or other forms of decorations. Installments meant to sell ones dignity. The choice was not random: the men of the Universal Church soon realized that these are the three items consuming most of the resources of their members.

Another method is to know how to award those who were worthy. The member showing the capability to communicate could become a worker. If he is good in gathering worshipers, he becomes an assistant pastor, then pastor of a small church and, if he distinguishes himself in his collections, he was going to minister services in the main temples. It was not an accident that three pastors of the modest church of Recreio dos Bandeirantes – Geraldo, Oswaldo and

Eduardo – were promoted to bigger churches after they found a lottery ticket called Grigore Avram Valeriu.

Grigore saw how important he was a little later, when he was providing his legal services as an attorney to the Universal Church. He took care of the documentation required for the owner of a building that wanted to sell it to donate the money to the church. In the taxi on the way to the bank was Grigore and pastor engineer Marcelo Crivella, later a Bishop, senator and runner for the government of the state of Rio de Janeiro. Crivella asked from which church Grigore had come. Humble, Grigore answered it was a small church, in Recreio dos Bandeirantes. Crivella then took from his briefcase a spreadsheet and showed that the temple of Recreio dos Bandeirantes was not that small. In 1989 and 1990 it was one of the churches that collected more money, surpassing many large and traditional temples. Grigore refrained from comment about this, but he knew the good numbers on the spreadsheet had an explanation: himself.

It came as no surprise that Grigore and Nadege ended up being "promoted". The then pastor Renato Suhuet, later a Bishop, took them to the church of Barra da Tijuca, larger and with more worshipers, saying that Recreio dos Bandeirantes was not a place for them. In other words: they had the qualities to be closer to the center of the faith. Their donation requests may have changed the methods but did not change the outcomes. Sometimes the money, received as checks and personal objects went into the little bag, other times it was over the open Bible. In Barra da Tijuca, the pastor used to feel more at ease to assure them that God told him donations of approximately six thousand dollars would appear. After this, he would tell them that he heard from the Heavens that three thousand dollars would come. And then 1,500, 1,000, 500 and so on, until everyone could be included in this weird means of income distribution, taking more from those with more and less from those who had less.

Their creativity and methods to fill the bags and gather worshipers had no limit. On New Year's Eve, all the churches near the beach had to carry out a gospel mission. Grigore was the leader of the Recreio dos Bandeirantes' gospel group, and wherever he went, he tried to persuade people that they would find fortune in the Universal Church. He was a convincing evangelist, even if in his case fortune was lost, not won.

On January 1st, the group was guided to erect a large white tent on the beach. Grigore's strategic role was to stay inside the tent, dressed in white from head to toe. On the outside, the members of the Universal Church – also dressed in white clothes – invited the bathers to hear the wise words of the man inside the tent. To those who went, Grigore talked a little about religion and handed over to the potential worshiper an address to go the following day, where they would find what they were looking for. In truth, not quite what they were looking. The sunbathers looked at the address Grigore gave them but they were not finding the church they heard about. They used deception. The church's scam was to be disguised of an African religion to attract those who were looking for it. Grigore knew the trick: when they got to the church, the sunbathers in fact found a Universal Church's temple, where they got the chance to be converted to the true faith. However, in this case, even the fanatic Grigore found it a little too much. He resigned as the role of the false African priest and in other years he did not take part in this charade.

That was the time that Barra da Tijuca saw one of the most creative campaigns to keep the worshipers attentive and enthusiastic. It was known as the Golden Book Campaign. The goal was to build the largest temple ever on a huge land site formerly owned by the state phone company. It would be one of the first Pharaonic constructions of the Church, and today still gets attention in the neighborhood of Abolição, in Rio de Janeiro. The building, bought from a furniture factory who had been the first Universal Church's temple, with capability for 300 worships, today is a 27,500 square feet with a capacity of 1,900 persons.

The worshipers who made donations for this noble cause would have their names written in the golden book. A thick book, obviously, with golden cape and the inscription Golden Book in brilliant gold, which would be buried in the site where the church would rise. The act, according to the pastors, would make those names eternal, so God would know who contributed to his work. Donations poured in. The book which contained thousands of names, among them Grigore's, is still there, buried under the Abolição temple.

The campaigns were successful strategies to attract worshipers around a righteous cause and, consequently, collect money. The time between one and the other were short. The Universal Church's members were always involved in some type of mission: Sinai Mount Campaign, Job Campaign, Ashes taken to Israel Campaign.

One of those actions, which mobilized many people, was the campaign to purchase a television network, Record, in 1991. The strategy was a collective engagement, the largest up to this point. Everyone together - worshipers, pastors, Bishops and workers – could buy a God's broadcasting station to oppose sin and degradation of the Brazilian people. Something they could watch on the Red Globo network. In opposition to the devil's broadcasting station, we would have a broadcast owned by the Lord, where God's people would have something to watch. The cause was a big one, and the pastors did not hesitate to ask the worshipers for everything they had to give, since this was an absolute priority. The pastors had to lead by example. They announced that the cars of the church were being sold. The Universal Church leaders would walk on foot, all in behalf of the Christian station.

Grigore was completely committed to the cause. He not only sold the car he just purchased but also sold his clothing store. Casa Marino was doing badly. The owner was spending more time in church than in the company. Worse, the employee in charge of taking care of the business started to steal clothing. The reason: the employee was a Universal Church's worker and stole clothing from the boss to sell to his colleagues, who needed uniforms not provided by the church.

This allowed the Universal Church to acquire their largest communication channel. It is possible that a few worshipers got frustrated, since years later Record would have a program schedule similar to that of its demoniac rival. The more similar it became in broadcasting soap operas formerly described by pastors as evil vehicles, the more Record was consolidated as the third most watched channel. The religious programs were broadcast during the later hours of the night.

Worshipers such as Grigore started to walk on foot. Bishops and pastors shortly after the campaign started to ride in better cars. For some people, the purchase of Record meant detachment; for others, the opportunity to get another car.

Some campaigns had less than noble goals. Grigore and Nadege once saw a night-watch, which made the Universal Church appear to conduct black magic rituals. Worshipers were called to establish a chain, directing their faith to cause the death of a rival of the church. The goal of the night-watch was told without euphemisms. Killing those who were in the way of the church was required, and the worshipers truly believed that those who were not with the Universal Church, at God's side, were in an alliance with the devil.

A few years later, even Grigore would be pointed out to be a friend of the devil. Through a few friends they still have in the Universal church, after Grigore and Nadege broke away, in a traumatic way, they were informed that the night watch for Grigore's death went on through the night, under the command of Pastor Randau Filho. Grigore was singled out as the man who dared to stand up against the Universal Church, and he deserved punishment. Who ended up having a tragic destiny was pastor Randau himself. During a trip to Japan, he suffered an accident and became quadriplegic. Heartbroken, he would commit suicide a few months later, according to information received by Grigore.

A Service in the Way

Grigore sold his real estate, one after another, believing he was on the right track to correct his life. Since that time the Universal Church did not accept donations of goods – due to the past difficulties to sell them – the worshiper should do this work themselves. If they wanted to give their car, land, house or any other thing, they would be responsible for the sale and only then would they give the tithe in money or check. The zeal of the flock was such that the Universal Church could have this luxury.

Grigore built his wealth mainly on real estate, which was never an investment characterized by liquidity. It was not easy to turn it into hard cash. Pastor Renato Suhuet offered to help. He went to the property with Grigore and kept praying so a buyer would appear. However, what really helped was not from spiritual laws, but from market laws. Grigore had to lower the price well below the real value of the property to manage to sell them quickly. The church was pressuring him to receive the donation quickly.

Other valuable goods that went for the little bag were the family jewels. First were those Grigore had bought for his wife. There were earrings, bracelets and rings, most of them made of gold and silver. Nadege liked them – after all, it was a gift contrasting with her personal history of few possessions. But what value had a whim – and even worse for material things locked in the safe of a bank – before God's call? Thus, the couple took the display case to the temple and they were very well received. They had given proof of their detachment. The same could not be said about Pastor Eduardo's wife, who from then on was seen wearing on her ears, wrist or neck some item removed from Nadege's display case.

The bank jewels, however, did not satisfy the pastor's appetite. He knew – because he shared the personal conversations of the members, who hardly kept secrets from the pastor – that Grigore guarded his mother's jewels. The jewels that almost made Nina stay in Romania, while the rest of the family waited for the airplane to take off for freedom. Those were not jewels forgotten in a bank safe, but were well guarded in the bottom of his emotional memory.

That was the approach the pastor used in his talk with Grigore. The jewels were linked to very bad times in Grigore's life. His mother, her attachment that almost got the family separated – an attachment Grigore could not inherit – the difficult childhood times in a watched country. It was the jewels that were hindering the life of Grigore, pastor Eduardo concluded. There were the heavy 22-carat golden rings, the heavy brooches with golden flowers. These were the only things remaining for the Hercovicis in their transition from Nazism to communism. They had to be hidden against the communist greed, which almost fell into the hands of the Romanian police. Now they went with little effort into the hands of the pastor of the Universal Church of the Kingdom of God. "The jewels did not go to the communist regime but went to Edir Macedo's regime", Grigore regrets.

And thus, from one sale to another, from donation to donation, his patrimony waned. In the expense column of the family budget, the highest entry was for the Universal Church. In practice, it was the same annoyances and mishaps through which a person whom lives with debts goes: checks he left in the little bag and was not able to pay, the pressure of the pastors – when not explicitly demanding payment – so that Grigore solved the problem, the routine bills delayed. Grigore and Nadege were going through their assets.

The worst point of the loss of assets wasn't the jewels, the properties, or the duns. Nothing they had donated compared to the moral and affective defeat. In spite of seeing his house with less and less furniture, making a living by loans and in the state of poverty, Grigore still considered the matter of honor the education of his children. Since the first school year, Gregório and Emiliano studied in a traditional quality college, called Anglo Americano, in Botafogo and with a branch inside one of the wealthiest closed condominiums of Barra da Tijuca. They grew with the best in terms of education. When their parents were living the Universal Church drama, the oldest one, Gregório, was attending the 4th grade, and the youngest one Emiliano the 1st grade. For the first time in seven years the school bill was overdue. The school was expensive, and everything Grigore earned – which became less and less – was going to church. Suddenly they realized they were three months late. Grigore and Nadege talked to the principal, who showed his concern but stood his ground: they had until the following Monday to settle the overdue payments.

It was a long and terrible weekend for the couple. They thought about all the possible ways to raise the money. To follow the opposite way, i.e. to borrow money from a Universal Church pastor, was out of question. Grigore had done that once. The answer was that helping a worshiper was not pleasant to God, because in case of any trial it was God's law that the worshiper should go through it.

The only possible solution was selling the car: a Maverick in precarious state. Grigore, who liked good cars, was acting in the reverse of what most people do. Instead of progressing from simpler cars towards the most sophisticated ones, to satisfy the Universal Church's desires, each time he purchased worse cars. The last of the series was the Maverick. Sold, in despair, below the valued price, which already was not high, but enough to cover the school debt.

With the cash in hand for the three-month overdue payment, Grigore Sunday morning went to the Universal Church to watch the worship services. After the emotion and purification, Pastor Renato Suhuet delivered a sermon speaking directly to Grigore's heart. As if he was reading what was going on in the head of his worshiper, the pastor said that donating to God is worth more than paying a debt, since God would return it twice over. In the pastor's mathematics, to leave the money in the bag meant the same as paying the debt and still receiving the same amount back. Grigore was hearing this with the school money in his pocket. He was praying, asking for a light. The pastor insisted questioning what was more important: the praise to God or debts, part of the worldly life?

Grigore was drawn into the pastor's appeal and his "prophecy" became true: The children lost the school year and had to go to a public school. The payment money stayed in the little bag.

The Path of Job

Without money, without goods, in times of need and with his marriage even worse than before he went to the Universal Church, Grigore rebelled. The opportunity was favorable. The campaign that led Grigore to storm Pastor Eduardo Cardoso's office, in Recreio dos Bandeirantes, was called a Revolt with the Devil. But Grigore's revolt had another address. In despair, he did not mind to blaspheme: "My revolt is with God, because I do not serve the devil." And he argued that during all that time he had donated what he had and what he did not have. He had given it all on behalf of the church with the promise to have it back in double. His investment was very high, and every time he said that to one of the pastors he received the same answer: Grigore had still not given enough to God.

Pastor Eduardo, however, chose a different approach. Grigore was being put in an extreme trial, the same path as Job, the biblical character. Job's faith became an object of a dispute between God and the Devil, which assured that Job only worshiped God because he had everything. There, when Job lost his flock, his daughter, his wife and his health. The boundaries of his devotion went to the extreme. Until that one day where he endured it no longer. Job lifted his arms to the heavens and cursed his destiny.

Exactly how Grigore was doing that afternoon, pastor Eduardo summarized. Instead of a victim, Grigore started to feel chosen. His fury was calmed. At last, it was not the first time that his life's path was compared with a Bible character, and that touched him deeply. His birth, at last, had similarities with history of Moses, the savior of the Jewish people who had to be hidden when he was a baby in order to escape being killed.

The trial in fact deserved the comparison with Job. Less than two years after becoming a worshiper in the Universal Church of the Kingdom of God, Grigore was now a poor man. In the church's bag Grigore left five apartments, four shops, a realtor, a clothing company, four cars - a Belina, a Del Rey, an Escort and a Maverick -, the family jewels, the jewels he had given to his wife, 14.7 thousand shares of the mining company Maranhese de Mineração, eight thousand shares of Lustrene and a good amount of hard cash.

"We went through the desert", Grigore explains. A desert where, paradoxically, at any given time during two days there was only water to drink. The refrigerator was completely empty. Grigore, Nadege and their two children went through times of hunger. When they had food, there was no money to buy gas. They were depending on the assistance of Nadege's sister or the solidarity of one or other worshipers splitting what they had. They also counted on the help of the Funds for Assistance to the Lawyers of Rio de Janeiro, after a protocol procedure where Grigore had to prove his bankruptcy.

From the apartment where they were living in Barra da Tijuca they went to a simple house in Recreio dos Bandeirantes. This repeated, with duns once again on their door and another eviction. "We got to the point of asking God to kill us and our children because we couldn't see a way out", says Nadege about the worst moments of despair. Even the humble childhood she had been far from the situation she was living, since she never was in need and there were always trees with fruits nearby in case of emergency.

The way out which appeared, turned out to be catastrophic. The entrepreneurship Grigore had early on shown signs of waning. The clothing shop on his property in Copacabana lost its head office to donations to church, and he tried to survive in a space rented in the Vila Isabel. It also ended up being sold for donations to the Universal Church.

During one of his many lamentations, Grigore received from pastor Oswaldo the suggestion to open a new business. After all, he had been a successful businessman, and maybe that would be the way out. The boarding house "Lá em Casa" offered, "domestic food delivery, made with care and fondness" for those who "work out of the home and have no time or simply do not like to cook".

The prices were good, but the menu sophisticated. From *vatapá* with rice, stroganoff with *souté* potato on Mondays to the roasted *carré* with rice and mayonnaise on Fridays, plus the traditional complete *feijoada* on Saturdays, Grigore, Nadege and a cook made an effort to take the business forward, working with only an old stove and a borrowed Kombi. The cook, by the way, was another victim of the exorcism rituals from the Universal Church pastors. He was one of many as a matter of fact. In all of them, the pastor cried out so that the demons that caused cook to have grotesque gestures would abandon him. The result was always temporary: a few hours later the cook's gestures returned.

"Lá em Casa" had many customers. The problem is that they all were pastors or workers from the Universal Church who ate for free. Grigore got some recognition as solidary to the congregation, but as businessman he failed.

"Jesus says that 'those who come to me come through love or through pain'. In the Universal Church, they all come through pain, sensible, hoping to find relief and peace. From there it is hard to turn into a fanatic", says Grigore to explain the brainwashing to which he was subjected. In the Universal Church, he declares, the low self-esteem makes everyone equal, whether a simple person, or a lawyer or engineer. The hope that tomorrow is going to be better, that suffering is going to cease, begins to be worth more than anything else. The promise of relief is expensive.

Devil's Advocate

In one of his talks with pastor Oswaldo, Grigore refused to hear the old history that the divine return for his efforts would come sooner or later. With the fridge empty, the children out of school, the wife restless, it was already too late. Grigore could not wait one more day to change that situation. Patience, trust in a higher power, submission to the higher will – all those sermons he was no longer willing to buy. He now wanted practical solutions. Like rising once again and preferably from that day on.

The pastor soon realized that his traditional speeches were condemned to failure. He then took another turn. During the talk, Oswaldo assured Grigore that he received a message from above pointing the way. Grigore got even more suspicious. After all, Suhuet seemed to have a direct line with some advising sector in the heavens, because he used to get so many messages. And worst: they usually were ineffective. Grigore politely reminded his interlocutor that the idea of the boarding house to sell lunch came from one of those signs, and the result only made his family situation worse.

But that time the pastor assured him that it would be different. The support Grigore required would need to be solid, something related to him. His soul was not in making lunch, but in the Law.

It started to make sense. The pastor's suggestion was great in its obviousness: considering Grigore was a devoted worshiper and a good lawyer, he should work in the legal section of the Universal Church.

Finally, Grigore found an answer that was unveiling the horizon. They planned the strategy: Grigore would speak to the head of the Universal Church in Rio de Janeiro, pastor Honorilton Gonçalves. Pastor Suhuet assured him he would schedule a meeting. Grigore went back home more at ease, as he hadn't been in a long time. When Grigore and Nadege arrived in Abolição at the date and time scheduled to speak with the praised pastor Honorilton Gonçalves – the man who makes the decisions in the Universal Church in Rio de Janeiro – they were surprised. There was already a long line on the outside of the temple, continuing inside of it, crossing all the rows of chairs, climbing a staircase to the upper floor and it kept going through the long halls until it ended at the door of pastor Honorilton. They were workers, unemployed, worshipers, beggars, housekeepers, all of them facing dilemma's just to have a word with the head of the Universal Church. It would certainly be brief and it was not even assured that they would get the chance. Pastor Suhuet confirmed that the time for meetings was always like that, but that the couple need not despair: Honorilton knew about their case and he would receive them without a line.

But it didn't mean with no waiting. Grigore and Nadege were placed into pastor Honorilton's room, where they shared the space with a group of pastors' wives that were getting a beauty treatment with a small group of professionals attending to them. They had to sit and wait.

Approximately two hours later, pastor Honorilton came in a hurry. There was the man who might save Grigore's life. Suhuet introduced them, and Grigore and Nadege received a cordial and distant salutation. While Suhuet was explaining their case, the attention of Honorilton was diverted by the presence of his wife, children and dog who had arrived. Grigore and Nadege only had exclusive attention a few moments later, already when Honorilton should answer: they could not hire Grigore as a lawyer for the Universal Church. The reason was not a bad curriculum vitae, lack of experience, expense containment or any other means to excuse a potential employee. In accordance to Honorilton, Grigore was not "freed". That means there was a malignant spirit bound to him and it was the cause of his failures. The only thing Honorilton could do, he assured, was to pray to get the spirit out.

On that day, Grigore took no excuses and left, willing not to accept cold treatment. On the following days, he returned to Abolição for further talks with pastor Honorilton, determined to make him realize the size of the problem he had ignored. In the first days, he waited for hours in the line he had feared. At the end of this pilgrimage, everything he got was always a brief word from the pastor in a hurry, assuring him there was nothing he could do.

After a while, the leader was not receiving him anymore. First it was with formal excuses and then with no excuses. Grigore adopted a new strategy. He discovered where Honorilton was parking his car and he waited for him leaning on it. When he had more time to express his drama – and that meant a few seconds more – he didn't mind asking, or to lose face and even kneel down. He insisted on a two-month trial experience, in which he could show how helpful he could be.

One day Honorilton finally surrendered. Possibly more determined to get free from the hindrance than for charity, the pastor told Grigore to look for the lawyer who took care of the Church's business in the state.

The Universal Church's legal department was located on the floor above the place where the radio Copacabana's operated. That moved Grigore in his first visit – after all, the voice that had established the course of his life had come from there. The starting point, which made him arrive, where he was at that time: the lowest point in the course. Now, maybe the upper floor was a metaphor for the future.

It was hope. Grigore would start as a legal adviser for the church, but it was already an improvement to his delicate situation. The salary was low. His routine job was solving an endless number of contractual problems that occurred. Debts not fully settled, renewals, small disputes, fines and other contractual quarrels, ranging from a line badly drafted to major failures. He received the case of a church he knew very well. The temple of Recreio dos Bandeirantes, his entrance door to the Universal Church, was about to be evicted. The reason: a year of rent was overdue. The church he had helped so much was not forwarding such help to the owner of the land. Now its future was in the hands of the former member.

Once again, Grigore would adopt the actions that were characteristic of his personality. He would be an impeccable and dedicated lawyer – the best one, as he had been in school, in college and in his previous jobs – even in less important causes. In the Recreio dos Bandeirantes eviction case, since the legal arguments were against the client, he tried other strategies: persuasion. He explained to the owner of the land that this was not just any common property, but the House of God. That the money certainly had been set aside to more urgent things: the spiritual work executed in there. The cunning was effective. Grigore got not only the pardon of the rents overdue but he also for a renewal of the lease agreement for one more year.

There was no case going to him that wasn't solved. He had one hundred percent success, which was noticed by his superiors. In four months, Grigore was head lawyer of the Universal Church in Rio de Janeiro. His earnings doubled, but it still was not very high. However, there were benefits. The Universal Church, for instance, was paying the rent of the place his new man of trust lived with his family. That was one more step above in his ascension.

The promotion was the incentive to make Grigore work harder. Now he not only solved many cases himself but he was in charge for the performance of the full department. The Universal Church's legal section lived its golden phase. Since they neglected contractual questions, there was plenty of work. The pastors from small churches living under the fear of eviction had relief. The Universal Church's safes saved the amount for fines that they would pay for not complying with the clauses. The sheep full of wool in the services had also sharpened their claws to assist in the legal area.

But the lawyer would not act as the worshiper. His head was not down as a sign of humility. Grigore knew very well his value, which he managed to preserve even after going through all those things. So he betted high with the intension to rise several steps in a single jump.

He looked again for pastor Honorilton in Abolição, but this time the level of the talk was different. Grigore was now a critical asset to the legal department. Perhaps the previous relationship in which he felt humiliated before his superior had an impact on his new attitude. The fact is that Grigore put the letters on the table very clearly, firmly and with confidence. He said that during the last several months he demonstrated his worth. He had proven to Honorilton that he would not regret giving him this opportunity. He was in summary a critical employee. The pastor was agreeing, not knowing where that man, who a few months ago, walked hunched over and transpired confidence. Grigore got to the point: he wanted the fulfillment of God's word in his life. That meant the prosperity the pastors repeatedly promised him since he entered a temple for the first time. In other words, increased wages, allowances and 5 million cruzeiros (around 6 thousand dollars) in advance so Grigore could put his life in order finally for that life he created after donating everything to the Universal Church.

Pastor Honorilton was horrified but he was also direct in the answer. For him, Grigore had gone mad. He argued that financial difficulties were part of the dedication to church, and that most of the pastors walked on foot. Grigore answered accordingly. "Sure, there are pastors who walk on foot. But many of them have brand new cars, as you do." And, to finish it off, he gave an ultimatum: he wanted to belong to the team of those who had prosperity, and he considered himself fully deserving of that. In case Honorilton did not accept his proposal, he would simply go away.

There was no agreement. Then go away, was the answer from the head of the Universal Church. Grigore knew he was retreating into dangerous waters, with no money and no expectations for the future, but he did not take it back. In the farewell, the pastor made an observation regarding the personality of Grigore: "One can say anything about you, but you are a man of faith." In that time, he had no idea of how that faith would cross his way and the way of the high administration of the Universal Church.

When he got home, Grigore had the reception he expected. Knowing that her husband had left his work, Nadege was infuriated. This was yet another serious fight in the history of the couple. She agreed with the pastor about her husband being mad. Despair times were again a way of life for the family.

Before the screams of his wife and with the world falling apart around him, Grigore did not argue. He just withdrew to his room to pray. He was convinced he had done the right thing and – more still – that the hand of God would help him.

He was not wrong. Less than a week later, a former colleague from the real estate agency contacted him with an incomplete message: "someone" had looked for Grigore there. That someone, who had left his phone number, was Pastor Renato Suhuet, who had just taken the function of the man who fired Grigore less than a week before. Pastor Honorilton was transferred to the Universal Church in São Paulo, and Suhuet was in charge in Rio de Janeiro. One of his first actions was to schedule a meeting with the former worshiper and former lawyer of the church.

They both met in Radio Copacabana and Suhuet asked Grigore to come back to work. The legal department needed him. Grigore was not intimidated by the week of bad expectations and family fights. He was assured that he would return if the same demands that had caused his dismissal were met. This time, he got a different answer. Pastor Suhuet agreed with everything, and the only negotiation proposed was that the 5 million would be paid in two installments.

The life of Grigore, Nadege and their children Gregório and Emiliano changed overnight. They were rich again. The church kept on paying the rent, not for the same apartment, but for a penthouse in Novo Leblon, a condominium in Barra da Tijuca. The children went to Veiga de Almeida, the school of Rio de Janeiro's cream of the crop. With the incoming money, the family that had walked for a long time on foot or used public transport bought two cars, not just any car: a Monza and a Comodoro in great shape. These cars were previously owned by the former Bishop Edir Macedo. He was the higher authority in the Universal Church. The Comodoro had a driver to take the children to school and Nadege to wherever she needed to go, which was usually shopping.

To enter into Grigore's well-decorated office– with good furniture and expensive carpet under his feet – was not an easy task. You had to schedule an appointment to see him, unless, of course, you were a member of the high administration of the Universal Church. Since he was paid handsomely, Grigore could be called any time of the day or the night, any day of the week, to remedy pending matters. The lawyer didn't care. He was living a brilliant time professionally and in his personal life, and he actually wanted big cases slamming at his door so he could demonstrate all his talent. Like a quarterback wishing to show his talents, Grigore was hoping the rival team would throw the ball against his cover.

Never could Grigore ever imagine that the throw would be so hard. It was Friday afternoon, time in which most of workers were planning on *happy hour* and the weekend. Grigore had the special privilege to go easy on Friday afternoons. After all, that had been the hardest week of work since he started to assist the Universal Church. He worked double shifts, as an employee and as a worshiper. They were at the eve of the great yearly service in Maracanã stadium. On the following day, more than 100 thousand people – who at that time should already been getting ready to catch the best places – would be jostled in the stadium to hear the words of the Church leaders. Especially from the supreme leader, Bishop Edir Macedo, who with his flaming and captivating speech closed the day in apotheosis.

But much work and effort were required before the apotheosis. The preparations started at least a month before. The endless legal and contractual matters to resolve overwhelmed Grigore and those below him. And his work was not restricted to the legal sector. As a dedicated worshiper, he was helping to disclose the event, he was doing campaigns and always ready to get his hands dirty in the organization.

That afternoon when everything indicated a lull in the preparations for the following day's service, the legal department of the Universal Church received an unexpected visit.

The president of the Universal Church at the time, Pastor Laprovita Vieira was one of the first to spread the Universal Church tentacles to other important strategic territories: politics. In the previous year, 1990, he had been one of three elected congressional representatives linked to the church. Pamphlets and banners with the numbers of the runners from the Universal Church were part of the services and sermons. Four years later the seats of the Universal Church doubled in the Congress. In 1994, the Universal Church was already a political power, with 26 assemblymen in eighteen states, 17 congressmen and 1.4 million voters. This was astronomical compared with the traditional mid-sized Brazilian parties such as PDT and PTB. In 2002, the Universal Church would lose a chair in

Congress, but would win one in the senate, with the election of Pastor Marcelo Crivella and the more than 3.2 million votes he received in Rio de Janeiro. In this legislature, the so-called evangelical group – a name given to the representatives linked to thirteen different churches – which had 60 representatives elected by 5.1 million votes, plus four senators. In 2006 the evangelical group members went to the same party, the Brazilian Republican Party – PRB.

That Friday, the pastor and congressmen Laprovita entered excited, into his office and a few minutes later asked for Grigore. He asked if he knew a lawyer from São Paulo called Celso Fachada. Grigore answered he didn't, and got intrigued not only with the question, but with the tension in the face of the president of the church. Then the bomb dropped. Bishop Edir Macedo got an arrest warrant and could not be present in Maracanã the following day.

Grigore did not ask why, or how, neither despaired. He simply went to the bathroom and prayed. After a few minutes, he came back and asked a question he considered critical: if that Celso Fachada, who was working on the case, was a Christian. He was willing to work this case, or better, he imposed that on himself with intensity and confidence informing Laprovita he would go to São Paulo to resolve the issue. For Grigore, it was not only of a legal matter but a spiritual one. The people would be deprived from hearing the so anticipated word of their spiritual leader, and to avoid that being a lawyer was not enough, it was necessary to be a man of faith. Grigore was both.

The president of the Universal Church was surprised and in doubt before that sudden enthusiasm. It was one thing to solve a routine civil concern – a thing he knew Grigore did well – it was another one to work on a criminal case, involving prison, testimonies, press and accusations Grigore knew nothing about. Grigore insisted he would immediately fly to São Paulo. Laprovita wanted to know why he was making that effort. "God spoke to my heart", the man of faith answered. It was enough. In general, a decision by the Universal Church was achieved only after consulting at least a half dozen other leaders. This time, Laprovita took this responsibility. Grigore was on the case.

Grigore had no time to go home first. He made two phone calls – one to Nadege, warning her about what was going on and another to the lawyer Fachada, asking him to wait for him. He left the radio station at 5 pm and one hour later he was boarding a plane in Santos Dumont airport. In the airport lobby he could see the drama into which he got himself into. The press was waiting for him, not only aware that he was on the case but with information Grigore himself did not even knew yet.

Celso Fachada was waiting for him in his house, a mansion in the neighborhood of Morumbi. The accusations against Bishop Macedo had come from a former ally and right hand man, Bishop Carlos Magno. When Magno left the church, in unfriendly terms, he went down shooting. He was a very dissatisfied dissident. Therefore, in that time, Grigore was not focused on the accusations, but on how he would solve the urgent problem: save the skin of the leader Edir Macedo. The accusations could be investigated later, since in fact the arrest warrant was due to the fact that Macedo had not complied with a call from the judge to testify to the Federal Police.

The colleague Celso Fachada calmed Grigore saying that the strategy was drawn. The plan was to take Bishop Macedo to Maracanã stadium the following day so he could show that he was a man of his word, and then he would go out handcuffed. That is right: the Bishop would be arrested with more than 150 thousand worshipers as witnesses, in addition to those watching it on the TV. There would be commotion, and the higher leader of the Universal Church would wear the uniform of the great martyr, God's messenger bringing the word of hope but sacrificed by the cruelty of man. And that, Fachada concluded, would be good for the defense.

When Fachada asked what the colleague thought of the plan the answer was: "Gee, you're crazy". Grigore did not waste time explaining, but this motto used by Universal Church members meant that the devil was using someone to carry out his intentions. In this case, to take Bishop Macedo to jail, this was ridiculous.

Thus, another alternative remained. Grigore proposed a simpler, however, more difficult solution: to annul the arrest warrant before the service. The difficulty was just there. It was Friday night and the courts were closed until Monday. For Grigore, the barriers did not matter. They would go to the house of the justice to present their case. It was not protocol, but it was the only thing possible.

Arriving at the house of the justice they only found his son, who informed them that his father had left and had no expectation on the time he would return. They left a message and waited.

At 1 am, they received the return phone call. But the voice on the other side tried to dissuade them, alleging that to speak with the justice at that time would not be a good idea. Grigore and Fachada would not accept this answer. They returned to the house and there they were informed the justice would not see them. They insisted that it was urgent. No excuse took Grigore away from his intention.

It was effective, but as expected. The justice appeared yelling, threatening to send them to jail for disturbing his peace. Grigore tried to argue, but the magistrate was not willing to talk, only to show his anger with these inconvenient lawyers. After he did that, he returned to the house not annulling the arrest warrant. In addition, they were hiding his state of drunkenness.

Fachada thought that it was the end, but immediately discovered that to give up was not in the plans of the colleague. Grigore insisted that he would only leave after the warrant was annulled. Maybe after a good rest and a shower the justice could give more attention to the case. Grigore was fasting, not only because he had little time to eat anything until that time, but as a way to strengthen the spirit.

Until 7:30 a.m. there was no saving movement; only the phone calls from Rio de Janeiro with Honorilton Gonçalves wanting to hear the news. Even on Saturday, Grigore thought, they might find a judge on duty who knows. They went out looking wherever there might be one of them. The search was effective. A judge of a court in the center of São Paulo heard the case with attention – in spite of the adversity of having to work on the weekend – he considered, heard the arguments – or better, almost appeals – of Grigore on the absolute need that Bishop Macedo could be in Maracanã a few hours later, that God's word could not be shut down, that the religious freedom should be assured. And, finally, he gave his decision: revoking the arrest warrant for 24 hours. Enough time to carry out the service and, then, continue the investigation. Grigore had just won one of the most important victories of his career.

God's Man in the Trunk

A few hours later, he has one of his greatest disappointments. Everything seemed to go well: Grigore called Rio de Janeiro, advised the president of the Universal Church, pastor Laprovita, and the head of São Paulo, pastor Honorilton Gonçalves, of the victory, they celebrated together by telephone and he heard that this was to be an unforgettable service. Grigore was feeling a fundamental part of that moment.

However, he and 150 thousand worshipers were surprised. Bishop Edir Macedo did not speak that day. The crowd who wanted to see him on the stage could not imagine that their idol was not there in Maracanã, but did not want to appear. Even with the prison revoked, Macedo preferred to be on guard. Hesitant until the last minute, he even came to the stadium hidden in the trunk of a car. There he remained hidden in a room of the centenary stadium. When it came time for him to speak to his worshipers, as the slang goes, he chickened out. The effort was in vain. Bishop Macedo did not manage to face his fear of being arrested and simply did not step onto the stage. Later he would go out the same way he came in.

If the course restrained in the trunk had been only to enter and leave Maracanã that would certainly be uncomfortable and somewhat humiliating. The problem is panic did not leave the supreme leader of the Universal Church, and on the following day he should go to São Paulo, taking care of business and, mainly, his defense.

When Grigore found his client the next day in a room at the house of pastor Honorilton in São Paulo, he was shocked. He was not a common client, but the man he most admired among all men on earth. God's representative himself, who Grigore thought would be capable of going through any trial, was lying on a bed, in a dark room, covered by a blanket and quivering. He confirmed he had got there after travelling 429 kilometers of highway with President Dutra in a place very different from his usual first class accommodations. He was riding in the trunk of the car.

The first image Macedo used to express his situation was that of a hunted man. In fact, there was a man backed into a corner, having a hard time to clear his mind and reasoning.

That meeting was not the first between Grigore and Bishop Edir Macedo. Every time they met in the administrative building of Rio de Janeiro, sometimes they changed greeting. Grigore had the chance to speak a few words with his idol when the Bishop brought to him the problem of a church they wanted to install in Campo Grande, on the western side of Rio de Janeiro, at the place of a movie theater they purchased. Due to a legal issue, the town hall had closed the operation. Grigore then pointed out to the shortest way to go through bureaucracy: a public petition. With 50 thousand signatures showing that the community wanted the church, it would be easy to persuade any politician.

Macedo promised all the signatures Grigore wished. That was not even necessary, political prestige of the Universal Church solved the issue.

The former confident man of that time was now depressed and pessimistic for his future. A spark only appeared after Grigore showed to him and to Bishop Honorilton the defense strategy. He assured Bishop Macedo that he would not go to jail. At this time, Grigore was considered the safeguard for the high administration of the Universal Church, primarily because of his repeated performance and knowledge of the law. The accusations against former Bishop Carlos Magno reached not only his former partner Macedo, but also other members of the upper hierarchy of the Universal Church: Honorilton Gonçalves, an Argentinean pastor called Ricardo Cis, pastor Randau – one who in the future would stand guard for Grigore, as well as his father – and their wives. Shots fired, not from a pistol, but from a machine gun, could hurt many people. Grigore was now the last resort. This was one of the most delicate times in the history of the Universal Church of the Kingdom of God and Bishop Edir Macedo.

In that moment, if someone could save them, that someone was Grigore. The plan, which revived the hopes of Bishop Macedo, was simply to take him in to testify. If the nonattendance of the Bishop in an interrogation by Federal Police was the reason for the warrant and arrest, then he should appear to provide an explanation of the Magno cases. It seemed easy, but there were obstacles to bypass. If Bishop Macedo was seen during his way to – or even at the door of – the Federal Police Station, he would certainly be handcuffed and perhaps taken away in a police car, with a chance for the press to grab a headline story. The arrest would come before any attempt of arguing. Therefore, it was important to meet the chief officer before encountering any police and, especially, before bumping into the prosecutor. It would make no sense that the chief officer ordered the arrest, for non-attendance, of a witness who was in front of him.

Inside the car on the way to the Federal Police, in the center of São Paulo, Grigore was once again advising Bishop Macedo how to behave during the interrogation. Using a language Bishops and pastors understand well, the direction was to "wear their Sunday Best". Pastor Honorilton added: "Don't get there with Friday clothes." Those metaphors referred to the characters the men of the Universal Church wear during their services. On Friday's the services were more eulogistic, with energetic pastors speaking loud, in dramatic exaggeration, dominating the worshipers with their strong and great presence. To wear their "Sunday Best" inferred a calmer, restrictive demeanor, as if the pastor was going to the Last Supper. They represented a good lamb talking with the worshipers in all their humbleness. It was being humble that would be a useful virtue at this time in the front of the chief officer.

They reached the door of the police station around 6 am. As expected, the gates were still closed. This was good for their plan, since they needed to enter without being seen until they got to the room of the chief. This was bad for the nerves of Bishop Macedo, who was increasingly nervous as time went by. While they were going around the block, the night without sleep and the days of pressure were weighing more and more on the back of the Bishop. This could damage his performance during the interrogation.

After driving around and making several turns, we finally saw lights on at the station and the door was open. That was the key moment. As if we were going to rob a bank, the vehicle quickly parked right next to the door and the occupants jumped out and rushed inside the building. A security guard informed us that we could not enter: the station was empty. He was the only one there. It was just what Grigore wanted to hear. With his license from the Brazilian Bar Association and his cunning nature, Grigore informed him that they would wait in the chief officer's room. They went in, watched by the frightened eyes of the security guard who had recognized the also frightened Bishop Macedo.

When officers, clerks, receptionists and, especially, the chief and prosecutor arrived later, they were surprised. The prayer they were hunting for was there; ready to talk about an accusation that was lifting so much dirt that not even the carpets covering the huge temples of the Universal Church could cover.

During the interrogation, Bishop Macedo behaved like a good lamb, following the directions he had received. He answered a few questions but, for most of them, he left his lawyer intervene to inform his client would answer that question during the trial. There were many pernicious questions, with the chief officer and prosecutor applying pressure, expecting that the evident jittering in the expressions of Macedo would gave him away.

Grigore, however, kept his calm with more effort than he expected. After trying so hard to calm his client, now he was the one afraid of betraying himself. It was during this tense interrogation Grigore finally learnt about the right dimension of sin knocking on the door of the Universal Church of the Kingdom of God.

The chief and the prosecutor talked about orgies held in hotels, at farms and in the mansion of Bishop Macedo. There were accusations of jewelry melted down into bars and sent abroad. There was also money that came from drug trafficking. According to the accusations of the former strong men in the Universal Church, four leaders were in Colombia with their wives. They came back with 1 million dollars from drug trafficking hidden in their underwear, used to buy broadcasting station time. The lawyer, who was expecting to find a formal accusation of charlatanism – an epithet that followed all history of Bishop Macedo – was now seeing the man in which he had unrestricted confidence being questioned about crimes immeasurably more serious.

There were so many details, psychological plays, new information and clever use of words by the prosecutor and by the Federal Police chief. Grigore had to make a tremendous effort not to ruin the strategy. The nervousness he feared in Bishop Macedo was rising within him. During the first hours of interrogation – from 9 a.m. to 1 p.m. – Grigore felt for the first time that his faith in check. During the lunch break, his concerns made him lose his appetite. The agitation was so apparent that the policeman responsible for watching Bishop Macedo joked that the lawyer was the one acting as if he had an arrest warrant for him. Macedo, in fact, seemed calmer, now confident he would reach his goal of leaving without handcuffs, a scene the press and a great number of persons were waiting to see on the outside. The case was in the news everywhere; it was the news of the day.

Grigore was more focused now on his inner drama than in the case itself. He was striving to convince himself that all of these accusations were just a great lie. Orgies? How was that possible, if the mission of Record was to build a God's broadcasting station, an antagonist to the erotic appeals of the diabolical Rede Globo? Trafficking and the Church? Definitely, those things could not be together. Grigore was sure it was a cruel blow to those carrying the truth, a fact repeated so many times in History.

He couldn't stop thinking about the ironic hypothesis of his family jewels being melted down. Before, who knows, they may have decorated the bodies of licentious women in great orgies.

Even with the conflict installed in Grigore's soul, he went ahead with his mission. With the shock, discernment was impossible. His faith could be on trial, and his task was to free his client and spiritual leader.

The testimony continued until 8 pm. Following the cold script, Grigore managed to avoid the trick questions and nullify the reason for the arrest warrant: the Bishop had appeared and collaborated with the investigation. Even then, the chief officer and the prosecutor did not give in. At the end of the interrogation, they declared that Bishop Edir Macedo would be arrested.

Before protests by Grigore, the argument was mixed with bureaucracy and ill will. It did not matter that the reason for the arrest no longer existed; there was an arrest warrant signed by a judge to be carried out.

To solve the deadlock, the solution was to go to the residence of the judge and try for dissolution. Lawyer Celso Fachada was in charge of this task, while the others waited. Fortunately, the judge worked nearby and the trip did not take long; unfortunately, he also was an enthusiast of bureaucratic procedures. To issue dissolution of the charges, he had to have proof in hand that the Bishop had testified. With great ill will, the chief wrote a statement confirming the testimony. Fachada once again went there and back and finally with the document granting freedom to the leader of the Universal Church.

The largest hindrance, however, was yet to come. Photographers, cameramen and live links to the nightly news were awaiting the exit of Bishop Macedo. A huge crowd took to the streets, cheering. The Universal Church was at a great disadvantage. The impression was that the restrained protest against the man who made millions from the faithful followers was now finding a chance to vocalize. The small number of worshipers awaiting the Bishop Macedo outside the Federal Police station couldn't be heard among the disgust of a majority of those screaming for justice against charlatanism. For those, the arrest of Bishop Edir Macedo meant a required reaction against the abuses of churches that exploited the weakness of the humble.

The group accompanying the Bishop tried to escape through a side street, but they were surrounded. As soon as Macedo appeared – in a moment which seemed like days – the microphones were pushed to his face, the light of the cameras were pointed at him, and the police barricade seemed too weak to contain the crowd. Grigore was walking right next to his client, in the tiny space they had to travel to reach the car. These were just a few meters travelled in victory of the first battle.

It was then that a loud noise and screams were heard, with frightened people of the crowd being pushed. A domestic bomb had been thrown, and nobody doubted who the target was. At that moment, Grigore became the guard of this man of God in those few meters of his way of his *via crucis*. With his body, he protected Bishop Macedo, convinced that if someone would die, that it would be

Grigore. With his reinvigorated faith, Grigore now felt that the Bishop was enlightened, a victim of the revenge of traitors. As a disciple crossing a Cross, that is the destiny of those who carry the truth.

At home, Nadege was watching everything live on the National News. The image of her husband protecting Bishop Macedo was also seen in the newspapers the following day. Fortunately, the domestic bomb was the tensest time of the night. On the way to the car, they were slowed by a few bags of sand that were part of construction in the street. These were nothing as serious as a bomb. They managed to arrive unhurt.

With the car in motion, far from the eyes of the chief, prosecutor, press and crowd, Bishop Edir Macedo started to cry. It was a crying very different from that Grigore had seen in the services, where Macedo used to show emotional outbursts. This one seemed more torn, more hurt, of a man totally out of control. In his mixture of tears with high moans, the Bishop complained that they were trying to destroy him. That what he was most afraid was that they would take testimony from him, like a valuable toy someone could steal.

It was during this purification; Bishop Macedo swore eternal gratitude to the man who saved him. Still in tears, he said Grigore would work next to him in São Paulo. With a tempting promise: Grigore would have everything he wanted. In that time, he was being promoted to guardian, right arm and one of the strong men of the Universal Church of the Kingdom of God.

Grigore thanked him, but did not accept the offer. He said he already had everything he wanted: family, children, comfort and the peaceful home he longed for so long. The children were adapted to college, Nadege liked Rio de Janeiro – he was feeling that this was no time for sudden changes. Macedo seemed not to hear the arguments. He just refused to accept no for an answer. Anyway, when the driver asked where he should take Grigore, the answer was direct: the airport. Grigore would go back home and talk to his family about everything that had happened, especially on what would come.

After solving the first part of the problem, Grigore headed back to Rio de Janeiro to be with his family. As soon as he entered his home, he received a phone call from the administration telling him to return to São Paulo, with the expressed recommendation to take a lot luggage because he could be required to stay a long time.

This time, Grigore went with Nadege, leaving his children – who at that time were 12 and 9 years old – in Rio de Janeiro. At the Congonhas airport, one of the best cars of the Universal Church was waiting to take them direct to the Record head offices, which at that time was near the airport. There they found pastor Honorilton acting very courtesy and attentive. This was quite different from the time when he refused to give Grigore a job almost a year before. Although he was busy – since at that time he was directing the live program 25th Hour, with debates and interviews regarding faith – he took care to insure that the couple felt at ease. When he was free from his duties, Honorilton went directly to the proposal to Grigore: Record director salary – 3 million and a half cruzeiros (equivalent to 13 thousand dollars) – a brand new car every year and a luxurious apartment in São Paulo to solve the Carlos Magno case.

The Faith Shaken

The Universal Church, under pressure, had no time to lose. The time for reflection they gave to their lawyer was minimal, virtually none. Grigore had time only to see his wife and his children one more time and to have a night of rest from the strenuous labor. The following morning, nine urgent and desperate phone calls came. The message was clear: they needed Grigore in São Paulo, for full and exclusive dedication to the Carlos Magno case.

That same night, Grigore returned to the São Paulo, this time with Nadege, moving in slow motion. He only had time for brief farewells and instructions for the children to place some clothes in his bags. The Universal Church said they would take care of anything else.

When they arrived in São Paulo, their first stop was C&A, a department store where they were authorized to buy whatever they needed. From the airport, where the tickets were waiting in the balcony, to a five star hotel, where a reservation was made, Grigore and Nadege found the doors open. Later, when they found a place to live in the neighborhood of Nova Conceição, near Ibirapuera Park and in a high class building of full floor apartments. Their moving and furniture expenses were paid in the most efficient way possible. The Universal Church left two blank checkbooks, only with the signatures, so the couple could use them as they saw fit.

The life project now was not only for that case, but always to defend the Universal Church. After the compulsory and hurried move, the Valerius blended in with the city. Even being in the half of the second semester and risking losing the school year, the children also came, and it was not easy to get a school transfer.

Grigore had minimal time to think about the brusque changes in his life. He routinely was taking care of the investigation, while at the same time had the role to calm down the high administration of the Universal Church. Macedo, Honorilton, Cis and Randau were consoled daily with their pessimistic and desperate crises. Bishop Macedo one day called him in despair to handle an urgent matter, a bomb that might hit him. Arriving there, Grigore was informed that there was a rumor that Carlos Magno was writing a book in which he would tell the full history of the Church. Grigore simply answered, "Let him do it", and amazingly that calmed the Bishop. It looked like all that he wanted was to hear a confident and sensible voice. The more Grigore assured them with this confidence, the more respect and responsibility he acquired. The book was never published.

On other day, there was pastor Honorilton Gonçalves the one who lost control. On the day of his testimony to the Federal Police, Grigore went to his house to pick him up. Honorilton greeted him with a mixture of shaving cream and blood on his face and went back into the bathroom. Soon Grigore understood why. Honorilton was shaking so much while shaving that he was constantly cutting himself, making the act look like flagellation.

In the car, Grigore advised him on the most important direction: notwithstanding that happens during the interrogation, Honorilton should stay calm. The plan backfired. In an explosive lack of control, Honorilton asked Grigore to tell him anything but that. Staying calm was impossible.

It was during this process that Grigore noticed a characteristic which was common to all leaders of the Universal Church of the Kingdom of God. This was a remarkable aspect of deep ambiguity. While on the pulpit, they were confident men, full of energy and faith, speaking with powerful voices and proud posture, behind the scenes they were weak men. The inability to take decisions was obvious, even the simpler ones. At any given time, for example, Grigore attended a meeting on the possibility of purchasing a movie theater in the city of Campinas to turn it into a temple. The decision dragged on for hours. As usual, Bishop Macedo consulted everyone, and this raised more doubts than certainties. The positions were hesitant. Everything was slow, done with indecision. During extreme situations in which they were living, the weak and frightened aspect of the leaders showed.

The honorable exception, says Grigore, was Pastor Marcelo Crivella, who later would enter politics. Graduated as an engineer and the son of a wealthy family, Crivella went through a history similar to that of Grigore in the Universal Church. As a worshiper, he lost everything he had in donations. Later he ended up in the group of highly distinguished pastors. He got rich again, achieving a standard of life that was even better than before. During the investigations, the couple Crivella and Marcelo and his wife Silvia were the only ones to keep their serenity and balance. Silvia is described by Grigore as a woman, polite and sincere in her intentions. During her interrogation, Grigore saw himself censuring the chief officer, who often crossed the line between incisive questions and disrespect.

At the end of the testimony, Grigore and the couple Crivella talked. Grigore confessed that the entire process was a disgrace to God's name. The scandals kept appearing. The Universal Church was suffering a deep wound, and that could not continue that way. The Crivella's were the only ones that saw the depth of the drama, and they defended it. It was time for the Universal Church of the Kingdom of God to undergo its own reformation.

Other leaders had a shorter vision. They wanted to avoid jail so that everything would return to normal. This coward position from the leaders made Grigore distrust more and more the attitudes of the Universal Church, although he avoiding thinking about that. It would mean to discover that everything he had believed was a huge lie. However, his efforts to divert his thoughts from this were put on trial. The faith that had been tested during the interrogation of Bishop Macedo was being shaken once again.

The worst episode was the very first meeting with Bishop Macedo in São Paulo. The place: Macedo's office, in the Record chairman's room. Grigore took Nadege so she could meet the great leader of the church. Their impression about the person was as suffocating as their impression of the place. That it would be a sumptuous and imposing office, they already knew. What surprised them was to see the carpets, the decorations on the table and the pictures on the wall. There were so many Greek statues with sensual nymphs, the abundance of Greek-Roman art. They immediately remembered the first pastor they had in the Universal Church, who destroyed their whole house on account of the same works of art. The critical rigidity only looks to be valid outside the Bishop's room. While Macedo was talking with the husband, Nadege scanned with her eyes from top to bottom. Not because she was praying, but because she was observing every detail of the enormous chandelier illuminating the environment, replete with figures of half-naked women. If their old apartment, described by pastor Geraldo as a den of sin and doom, then Bishop Macedo's room was truly hell on Earth.

This was a contradiction that was hard to forget. One more of so many following Grigore during the three months he devoted himself to defend with exclusivity the Universal Church from the more serious accusations they had suffered. He went to work in an office right next to Bishop Macedo's luxurious room. Every day Grigore lived with the enigma on the other side of the wall: Was he defending God or the Devil?

The pendulum strongly pointed to the latter the day he attended the testimony of Pastor Ricardo Cis, the Argentinean who knew everything about television, and thus was the person in charge of the entire technical section of Record. On the day of the interrogation, he showed the same panic attack as the others. In his case, it was with intense agitation.

Because the prosecutor was late, the chief officer decided to go bully and reminded Cis that he was arrested. Grigore opposed to this arbitrariness, but the chief officer had woken up uncompromising that day. Grigore then changed the tactics: if his client was going to be isolated in a room, he would not be alone – Grigore would go with him. The chief officer argued that the Pastor was arrested, not the attorney. Grigore insisted and complained so much that he got what he wanted: being arrested also.

Both of them stayed in a room in the Federal Police station, without communication and with a policeman at the door. The time in that unusual arresting would be the time the prosecutor was late. They ended up there for two hours. Enough time to make Pastor Ricardo Cis collapse start to cry, a scene to which Grigore was getting use to with the men of the Universal Church. He proposed that they pray together. The prayers were growing in emotion until they turned into songs. Under the curious looks of the policeman, both were carrying out their particular worship.

Amid the thrilled crying, Grigore took courage to determine the ultimate question. He did not want to spend any more days in the crossroad, in the doubt on which was the way of the truth. Grigore asked if, in the name of God and of conscience, the facts in the proceedings were true. Pastor Ricardo Cis, in an explosion of honesty, confirmed everything.

After a silence, the confessor, a little more prudent, pleaded to Grigore to keep that discussion to himself. There were things which could not be said, the pastor assured. Grigore agreed. Then, they proceeded to the testimony and Cis left the Federal Police station free. Not before, like the others, swearing gratitude to the lawyer who had saved him.

From the same room that challenged Grigore's understanding, came the final blow. During a meeting behind closed doors, Bishop Edir Macedo and Pastor Honorilton Gonçalves told Grigore they had a strategy to solve the problem. Grigore found it weird. After all, until that time, he was the only person proposing solutions. The strategy of the defendants consisted more in running like frightened cockroaches than any other rational behavior. But this time they seemed convinced.

The plan was very clear. Grigore would look for the judge in charge of the case and ask how much he wanted to declare the leaders of the Universal Church innocent. The lawyer would have a free negotiation margin: the amount asked by the judge would be paid. If in addition to the money he wanted some whim or guarantee, he would also receive. In summary, everything the judge wanted would be delivered.

Macedo and Honorilton's feeling seemed sharp again. The judge in charge of the Carlos Magno case had an aspect more similar to a rock musician than of a magistrate. It was easier to see that long white haired man on the stage wearing black clothes and singing 1970's hits than behind a board coordinating a trial. It is not possible to know if the leaders of the Universal Church thought that everyone has their price or if they had some information – or even hint – that that judge would be especially sensible to a corruption proposal. João Carlos da Rocha Matos would in the future play the lead role in a scandal called Operation Anaconda. Being the central figure, in a business, in which the product was the sale of judicial sentences, federal judge Rocha Matos would end up in jail in November 2003.

What Macedo and Honorilton were not counting on was that, even if Rocha Matos were corruptible, Grigore was not. The lawyer answered that he would not carry out such a task, and he did not stop there. As if he were unloading a huge bag of doubts, accumulated against, and regarding the honesty of the leaders of the church, Grigore began a speech against that kind of attitude. An inflamed speech, as if a jury could hear it. No longer defending, but attacking the Universal Church of the Kingdom of God. He was aiming for their strongest men.

Grigore reminded Bishop Macedo that his sermons indicated that God would always bring solutions and protect the just. How could he be afraid? Did Macedo have a reason to be afraid? Does the truth not always triumph over lies? Was not God's justice implacable? The words Bishop Macedo use to utter to the worshipers were now used against him. The whole contradiction of his faith was questioned. Not only by a lawyer, but by a worshiper as well.

Bishop Edir Macedo and Pastor Honorilton Gonçalves watched the scene in silence and were horrified. They probably were not expecting to hear such a sermon, to come across anybody demanding coherence between their preaching's and practices in life. Going one-step further, maybe they never figured someone would demand truth in what was said within the temples of the Universal Church.

After the end of the speech, Macedo looked to Honorilton slowly shaking his head and showing a cynical smile. Something that could be translated as, this guy is a fanatic; he is not one of us. Then, he stood up and went out.

Grigore's journey as a man of trust of the Universal Church of the Kingdom of God ended there. A new road lay ahead with a steep downward journey: the journey of a *persona non grata*.

Stare Duel

The following day he received a notice telling him he was transferred to the temple of avenue Celso Garcia, in the neighborhood of Brás. Here he was placed in a small room, wet due to infiltration. He was definitely off the Carlos Magno case.

Grigore had to follow from far away what would be the decisive moment of the investigation. The Federal Police would promote a confrontation between the man who made the accusations and Bishop Edir Macedo. The former partners and now mortal enemy face to face to discover who had the truth.

A time that was promising to be the climax of the process against the Universal Church turned into a maximum anticlimax. Carlos Magno simply did not appear. Which brings into question: Why someone who had gone so far, with the heaviest accusations against the Universal Church had received until that time, simply disappeared on the day he could confirm them? Magno went back in the most decisive moment, in a quite suspect behavior.

Grigore now was observing from far away, but without a lot of interest. His case now was different. He was defending himself in search of justice. Thus, he looked for Bishop Edir Macedo, convinced that the talk they had never ended. The Bishop avoided him any way he could. The various exits in the Universal Church temples – in order to avoid such meetings with unwelcome persons – were a great weapon. Grigore watched the services of the man who had sworn eternal gratitude to him and soon he would see a worker looking to him, who certainly would tell the boss to use the emergency exits.

One day Grigore managed to interrupt the escape route. The meeting he was expecting with Bishop Macedo – face to face – happened in a wide corridor leading to the stage, where a service was waiting for him. Macedo said he was in a hurry, but Grigore was not willing to give in to the Bishop's excuses. Blocking the way, Grigore tried to bring the man whom he had trusted so much to the light of truth. He argued that there was still time for a change, a time to repent, that there was still time to correct the mistakes. Moreover, that the Universal Church and his leaders could find again the way to God. In synthesis, Grigore acted as a Pastor, and Bishop Macedo would be the sheep to be saved.

The sheep, however, was not interested at all in conversions. What h heard seeming boring and he did not answered. After Grigore ended his speech, the Bishop walked by and went to minister the service, never saying a word.

With his salary decreased by half and with the Universal Church no longer paying the high rental of the apartment where they he was living with his family and the car installments – i.e. no more meeting the promises made – Grigore saw his future tightening up. Even thus, he continued his work in the wet room at Celso Garcia. He was now back to working on contract issues and out of great causes.

It wasn't until he was called to a meeting with the administrative leaders of the church from several cities of Brazil and with President Laprovita Vieira that he found out the goal was to plug a drain through which much money was being lost. There were fines, contractual faults and non-compliances in general that were drying the safes and deserved special attention.

Labrovita showed the day's schedule and introduced doctor Grigore to the person who basically would guide them to stop losing money with silly things. Grigore took the word, and ended up expanding the size of the problem to an uncomfortable field for Laprovita. Grigore said that many churches were disgracing God's name. Every day the news showed accusations of illegal operation, lack of permits, irregular constructions. He further stated that the Universal Church was working on the border of illegality, contradicting the ethical behavior it preached in the services. The surprise of the attending leaders was proportional to the embarrassment of the president. Grigore also mentioned the images in television news of a church sealed by the public authority of Jundiaí, due to non-compliances. "The Universal Church is reviling in the name of Jesus", he concluded.

The following day, upon receiving the dismissal notice by the head of Celso Garcia, Pastor Romualdo, Grigore kept on playing hardball. He warned that he would only leave if Bishop Edir Macedo fired him personally and acknowledged the reason for the termination.

Romualdo knew the willingness of his employee to fight and barely discussed it. Two hours later, he came in again to say the Bishop was waiting for him. The first thing Grigore asked Bishop Macedo what violation he committed to cause the termination. "You are not obedient", he answered, according to Grigore. The retort: "Thank God I am not obedient to your requests, but I am obedient to God." Grigore alleged he was only carrying out his duty as a lawyer when he demonstrated his non-compliance to the Universal Church's agreement. Insulted, Bishop Macedo drew his favorite weapon, the Bible. While he was leafing through the pages, he assured he was going to show that God's word would give him endorsement that he was not required to open legalized churches, which could take a long time. He found his alibi in the Proverbs of Solomon: "Be not righteous over much; neither make thyself over wise." In context, the sentence was advising the use of common sense. Even for using justice and wisdom a balance should be found. In the very particular interpretation from Bishop Edir Macedo, the prophet Solomon was legitimizing trickery. As a matter of fact, this skill to manipulate the scriptures according to their purpose was always one of the outstanding characteristics of the Universal Church, soon mirrored by the new evangelical churches.

Grigore accepted the fight and indicated that God would show he was right. He reminded Macedo that the Universal Church was the one not complying with the work agreement, on account of the promises for which he had come to São Paulo and now he was in a quite sensible situation. He reminded the Bishop about the vows of gratitude in moments of despair.

The furious stare of Bishop Macedo indicated that he was willing to set forth one more weapon. During the services, Macedo boasted that with a simple stare he could frighten the devil from the body of any person. His firm stare was enough and the possessed person could not stand the stare. Nobody who had sinned in their heart would manage to face him. The defeat would be simply by the lowering of their face. The fame of the Bishop Macedo's stare was thus that the possessed person would fall backwards upon meeting his stare.

Therefore, the Bishop decided to set aside the oral argumentation and to go face to face. Grigore accepted the fight. They were for long seconds one next to the other, in a staring duel, in which the one who looked away first would be defeated.

In the end, Bishop Macedo lowered his eyes, closed the Bible and walked away. Grigore took the opportunity to say that he was not even a bit a man of God: he was a man with no words and no morals.

Open Doors, Closed Doors

Even after receiving his dismissal directly from Bishop himself, Grigore kept on refusing to be fired. On the following day, he worked as if nothing had happened. His conviction that the termination was unfair made him simply ignore the orders from above.

The following day he went to work, but this time the method was different. His room was closed and his things were outside (missing a few personal objects Grigore never got back). The message was clear: it was not only about termination; Grigore was expelled from the Universal Church of the Kingdom of God.

A curious fact is that on the day he found his office doors locked, the Church was quite busy with other campaigns. The one consisting of prayers, sermons and watches so the worshipers could find a job. The pastors were assuring them that after that day a placement in the labor market was going to surely happen for those taking part in the service. To symbolize this new time, a door was placed on the pulpit. Going through this door meant they were on their way to a new job.

It was the Open Doors Campaign.

The reality of having his name in the *index* of the enemies of church did not take long to appear. During the following, the former employee could only fight for his labor rights. The Universal Church was not willing to concede even that. 'Come here another time" was the information he received every day.

While the time was going by, the foggy shadow of poverty past surrounded his family once again. The Universal Church forced they out of their apartment, there was neither money for the car payment, nor for the children's school. The family had assumed a high living standard that was quickly consuming their resources. Money was merely going out and not coming in. There were almost no reserves, simply because the donations continued while he was an attorney for the Universal Church with a high income, and in the proportion of what he was earning.

Soon bankruptcy was becoming a reality again. To avoid seeing his children hungry, the couple did not wait to send them to the house of her sister, in Juiz de Fora. Their brother-in-law worked as a salesman and was living in a low middle class standard, which at that time was better than what the parents could offer.

While at Celso Garcia, he could not even manage to talk with anybody in the church, Grigore went to straight to the Record station. There he looked for the technical director Ricardo Cis. Unfortunate for Bishop Macedo, Pastor Cis showed gratitude for the solidarity in the hours of the arrest. He assured him he would resolve Grigore's work issues, which would give him a fresh start.

They both went to the Celso Garcia temple. Grigore waited outside while Cis entered to talk about the concern. He left disheartened. In spite of having found someone with good will, the obstacles of Grigore were much greater. Embarrassed, Cis told him he could do nothing, and that the Universal Church's direction forbade him to get involved in the case or even keep contact with him, as if Grigore had a serious contagious disease. That would be the treatment he received from there on, whether by the conviction of those pastors or because nobody wanted to contradict orders from the church superiors.

Cis still tried to help within his abilities. He invited Grigore to have lunch in one of the most traditional barbecue restaurants of São Paulo. Grigore was hungry, but declined the invitation, explaining that he would not feel good having plenty of food in a barbecue restaurant while his wife was waiting at home with an empty fridge. Thus, the last resource of the pastor was to pull out all the money he had in his pocket and hand it to Grigore, wishing him good luck. It was not great, since a pastor usually paid for everything with unlimited credit cards. Grigore does not remember exactly the amount, but he thinks it was the equivalent of 30 dollars – 0. 25% of the wage he was earning as a lawyer.

He left with the option of giving up on the upper administration of the church and sought help from humbler people linked to the Universal Church. Grigore remembered a friend he had in the Record station, known by everyone as Mr. John, a typical old man who always had his hand extended for those in need. The friendship between Grigore and Mr. John started around charity. While they were waiting for the beginning of a service by Bishop Edir Macedo, Grigore and Mr. John – also a Universal Church's worker – sat down side to side. A man appeared to speak, wearing torn clothes, calling himself a father and asking for help for his children and wife who were hungry at home. Grigore calmed him down, and Mr. John volunteered to speak to the pastors. Returning, he informed Grigore they should not help. The pastors told: we teach them how to fish; we do not give them fish. In dismay, Grigore and Mr. John gave him what they had in their pockets. The man left a little more relieved. Grigore and Mr. John watched Bishop Macedo's sermon on fishes and fishing. They then shared the complicity of going against his recommendations.

This time Grigore certainly did not want Mr. John to give him everything he had in his pocket. The contribution could be more modest however more valuable. Mr. John was the person in charge of the TV Record programming, taking care of maintenance. All Grigore needed was gas. The idea, at that time, was to go back to Rio and restart his life.

Mr. John, as expected, filled the tank of Grigore's car, of course. He did more. The things to taken on the trip were minimal. Grigore had come to São Paulo with hardly anything and was going back likewise. The apartment where they lived was already furnished. The only things the couple had were a sofa and a television set. It was little, but they did not fit in the car. Mr. John volunteered to go with them to Rio in a Van – not one from the church, but his own – and help in the moving.

That was how Grigore and Nadege returned to Rio and to ground zero, with Mr. John Van following them with a few extra stops due to mechanical problems. Then they stopped in Juiz de Fora, to pick-up up their children.

Back to the Start

Grigore intended to close this chapter in his life once and for all. Forget that at one point he was a member of the Universal Church of the Kingdom of God. But for that, a dispute needed to be resolved. He had left with nothing, and he needed his labor rights to rise again. He was aware that it would not be an easy task. Firstly, due to the depth of the ill will demonstrated by his former bosses. Secondly, that Grigore has worked with no formal contract of any kind. He provided his services trusting the words of Bishop Macedo and the high pastors, who now were worth nothing. Anyways, as a lawyer he knew that even though he had the right to obtain benefits such as social security, notice, proportional vacation payment – since no doubt remained that he and the Universal Church had an employment agreement. However, his opponent would not help in any way.

When they reached Rio de Janeiro, there was no money to rent an apartment. Therefore, they had to go to the house of Nadege's other sister in Jacarepaguá. Very early the following day, Grigore went to the Church of Abolição to speak with the cousin of Bishop Edir Macedo, Mauro Macedo.

Although related, they were so opposite in character. Mauro Macedo was not a pastor and did not attend the services. He didn't talk much about God and Jesus, but he took care of the administrative part of the Universal Church with much more competence than any pastor. Grigore describes him as the smartest man in church, also having a good heart. Mauro listened to Grigore's story and lamented. He already knew a little of what was going on, but not the depth of it. He came to the same conclusion Grigore had arrived at already: he should never have left Rio de Janeiro; in São Paulo things were different. The high administration of the Universal Church, the head offices of Record and all financial transactions were coordinated in São Paulo.

Anyway, Mauro pledged himself to solve the issue. His actions were proof. That same day he gave Grigore a sum of money, and asked him to come back in two days for the remainder.

Grigore returned, but the money was not there. On the other hand, the good news was that the Universal Church was not looking that uncompromising. According to Mauro Macedo, the direction was that Grigore filed a labor dispute – with the issue that it should be conducted in São Paulo, jurisdiction of the defendant's head offices –, then he should enter into an agreement with the attorney of the Universal Church and, in front of the judge, they should establish an agreement to close the proceedings. In summary, the Universal Church would pay, but it wanted legal reassurance that Grigore would never return to give them problems.

Thus it was done. With a plane ticket paid for by Mauro Macedo, Grigore returned to São Paulo. In the city, he spoke with his former colleague doctor Maria, from whom he received a written agreement. In summary, the text indicated that the agreement concluded all disputes between Grigore and the Universal Church.

Two days later they were called by the judge to ratify the agreement. Grigore left with no great fortune, but with some money to continue his life. And to continue with no more contact whatsoever with the Universal Church of the Kingdom of God. For him, that was the end of the road.

CHAPTER 3 - PARADISE

Familiar Jury

While for Grigore his history with the Universal Church had reach the end, for his family there was still a long journey ahead. The name of the church and of Bishop Macedo was present during the Valerius meals for a long time.

Grigore, even though he was unemployed, was satisfied with the payment he received, which allowed to him to rent an apartment in Barra da Tijuca and gave him enough until he found a new job. That was not easy at all. He was out of the Rio de Janeiro market for three years, enough to lose contact with former clients. Worse, the returned to Rio de Janeiro in February, a time in which the summer heat and carnival freezes the labor market.

Additionally he was a lawyer without an office. To rent an apartment had already been hard, because it was impossible for him to prove stable income or get a guarantor. They ended up finding a place in a condominium in Barra da Tijuca that accepted them as tenants since they paid rent in advance. An office would be a luxury at that time, but the lack of it would make it hard to practice as a lawyer.

The solution was to resort not to new clients, but to old acquaintances, persons for whom Grigore could tell of his situation and who got him sporadic jobs. Practicing law became a sort of temporary job, solving contractual issues here and there and providing consultancies. It was unstable, but it was something.

My wife and children, however, were not satisfied at all to see me in this situation. They were unanimous in repeating that the high injustice of which they were victims could not be left without reparations. The children Gregório and Emiliano had grown enough to fully understand what had happened and, mainly, to complain. In time, they were able to laugh at past embarrassments. Such as the day when their father picked them up at the school with a cement grinding truck. For the children, it was the embarrassment of the year with them being mocked by their school friends for a long time. It also caused Gregório to lie telling them that his father was an engineer. For Grigore, that was the only possible solution, since he was driving a Fiat 147 borrowed from a friend which broke down every time it stopped. At traffic lights, Grigore needed to drive as slow as possible without stopping the vehicle. When he was arriving in the building garage, he had to hit the horn from far away so the caretaker, knowing the problem, would open the garage gate in advance. Traffic jams were fatal. On that day and with the car once again having let him down, Grigore looked for help at the gas station. This is where he found the cement truck driver willing to help this zealous father.

Now, even today, these comic tales are merely a tenth of the emotional and affective chaos caused by the Universal Church. Nadege also agreed that such history could not be left without an answer. The church had taken from them their peace and all the goods they had. It made them poor and full of scars in the soul. Now they had to restart their lives from nothing, for the leaders of the Universal Church, life continued to be wonderful. The bitter taste increased every time they watched the night services of the Universal Church on TV Record, with testimonies of people who went from nothing and achieved success. Grigore and Nadege periodically recognized a pastor from the church of Madureira pretending to be a successful businessman who got to the Universal Church without preconceived notions, or people near to the higher ups making an appearance and indicating that they were previously disturbed and have found a way. There is justice in their deceit, a provocation to everything they believe: that in the end justice always prevails. In the family jury Grigore was losing 3 to 1 from the votes of Nadege, Gregório and Emiliano: they wanted Grigore to sue the Universal Church of the Kingdom of God. Grigore was a lawyer and was in his right, then why not? Before the resistance, they were not hiding their opinions that Grigore was being stupid.

For Grigore there were several reasons for resistance. One was that they didn't want to go through that drama again. The other was that he didn't want any more trouble. He saw the Universal Church as a problem of the past, while the rest of the family saw it as a problem of the future.

Anyways, he heard their opinions and thought about it in the same way that he was accustom when facing a sensitive decisions: he prayed. Talking to God, he was looking for direction from the top. In spite of all difficulties he had in his spiritual path, Grigore's faith became stronger, instead of weaker. In spite of having found charlatans in his search for the divine word, he did not abandon his religious nature. On the contrary, he started to live it deeper. From everything he had lived, he could differentiate what was really from God and what was the work of men.

The prayer period was long, a little more than eight months. Then he took a decision not guided by an inner voice, as it is usually told about those who retire to meditate on a subject. Grigore tells that the voice was from outside of him, and mighty, since the decision to sue the Universal Church was given to him by God.

In one of the prayers it came to him with the power of the words of the gospel of John: "The thief cometh not, but for to steal, and to kill, and to destroy." He didn't need to go far to see the destruction the Universal Church had caused in his life. He was seeing the thefts every day, with housemaids and workmen leaving with almost nothing but what they had in their little bags. About death, he remembered several cases where he heard of worshipers who committed suicide after the devastated in their lives that came after becoming a member of the church.

Maybe it was time someone should testify about the truth, unlike the fraud they broadcast at Record. Maybe someone needed to tell the real histories of a person who became a member of the Universal Church? Histories like that of Grigore, who had a history completely different than the standard "I came with nothing and became wealthy".

And that was how he started, as he woke up at 5 a.m. while his family was sleeping, and began to write the initial petition, for ten nights. In his head a movie played recalling the full history of his life, while his hands wrote without stopping. "The words were coming by themselves", says Grigore, in what he called divine inspiration.

Biblical Suit

God's will, according to the "prophets" of the Universal Church, is that the members should detach themselves from material items, from cash, donating everything they have through the tithe, the doubled tithe or triple tithe, donations and sacrifices such as the full month salary, money for debts, for rent, house keys, car, telephone, all jewels, donations of lots, lands etc., and obtaining, with the guarantee of the "prophets" themselves, the assurance that God would then reward them with spiritual peace and financial blessings immeasurably above the amounts donated.

They use, as a permanent slogan, that there is only one way to prove oneself to God: through the tithe and donations, invoking and showing, invariably, the word of prophet Malachi: "Bring ye all the tithes into the storehouse, that there may be meat in mine house, and prove me now herewith, saith the Lord of hosts, if I will not open you the windows of heaven, and pour you out a blessing, that there shall not be room enough to receive it." (Malachi 3-10).

But, Your Excellence, that tricky and fake history invented by those "prophets", adapting God's word to their greed and mean financial interests, is quite different from the true biblical history and whose revelation was recently made by the Lord to the Petitioner through his study of the word.

The initial request presented by the lawyer and petitioner Grigore Valeriu was one quite uncommon in legal environments. Instead of quoting eminent jurists to corroborate a point of view, experts who weigh in to the argumentation or even classic cases serving as comparison, Grigore appealed to the Bible. Instead of the cold and objective text that characterizes legal drafting, Grigore often used adjectives, emotional pictures, subjectivity. For him this way was the only possible way. He had his own interests, and as lawyer representing himself, could not impose the distance generally characterized as the lawyer-client relationship. Additionally, the process would only make sense if he entered the subjectivity of the facts, since what was being considered was a life history. That was about rescuing all goods he had before being a member of the Universal Church – plus compensation for moral damages. The value he estimated in the process was equivalent to approximately 600 thousand dollars.

It was required to show the mechanism that leads a person to become removed from his own will, from his clear discernment. He needed to show how the Universal Church of the Kingdom of God was able to get their worshipers in that state, using means so complex and wicked in order to finally led those sheep to ruin.

It was not an easy task. At that time the Universal Church scandals were already known by society, with a good part of the so called opinion formers automatically associating the Universal Church with theft through faith and Bishop Macedo to charlatanism. But to prove it in court was other thing. How to show the sins of the Universal Church if judges are trained to consider no value judgment, no subjective criteria, only favoring the facts?

Another difficulty, one which should not be neglected, was that Grigore would face a power immeasurably stronger than him. He was going to battle alone against a full army which he could count with the best soldiers. Certainly the Universal Church would have at their side not one, but a body of the most renowned lawyers willing not only to refute the petition but to find anything which could be turned against Grigore.

To win he had to fight with his weapons. Therefore he would use his emotional and biblical tone. He should show that God's word was being unjustly used by the pastors of the Universal Church. His request was at the same time a legal instrument and a faith instrument.

In the case of the passage of prophet Malachi – the main verse in the Bible confirming authority for the infinite donations during the services – Grigore was quick to reveal the correct content and context:

Malachi was the last of the prophets to talk to the Jewish people, in their own land. When he wrote the words quoted, a hundred years or more had passed from the return of Jews to Jerusalem, after the Babylonian Captivity. After a period of revival (described in Nehemiah 10:28-39), people became cold regarding religion and morally neglected. By neglecting the House of God, and not delivering the tithe and the donations and thus justifying prophet Malachi to courageously challenge them saying: "Will a man rob God?" (3:8), and the call to them to bring again the tithes and donations, creating then the opportunity to, after proving to God that they obeyed, be blessed by Him.

Thus, the history adapted by the "prophets" of the Universal Church is exposed as a fraud by the biblical history that teaches the true meaning of the word 'prove' in Malachi 3:10: to show God that the people were fulfilling their obligation with Him.

It was a matter of putting order to the chaos of the gospels created in the hands of the Universal Church leadership. The Bible was used to collect money in a metaphorical way and also directly: it was through their words that the worshipers were persuaded and, often, the money was deposited on the sacred book itself, which circulated open in the hands of some of the worker in charge of receiving the donations.

In addition to the twisted use of the biblical words, Grigore decided to go beyond, showing that the true word of God not only did not justify the church's actions but also against them.

Nevertheless, the petitioner continued to assiduously attend the services and praying to God to show the leaders the truth and to change their thoughts, as well as the greed and pleasure with which they were shearing the sheep, i.e. forcing the members, by coercion and emotional blackmail, like "who loves to God has to prove it, giving everything", to give away their material belongings and literally live in misery, as in fact did live most of the members, workers and even the pastor of the church of Recreio dos Bandeirantes, attended by the petitioner at the time.

It is important, for the truth, to point out a major aspect: pastors are recruited, or better yet, pastors are chosen amongst the church members after undergoing a worker's traineeship. Education was not a requirement.

Most of them are persons who deeply love God and piously believed in what they preached to the worshipers and in the direction given by the church. This direction led to a life of deprivation and trials, while the leaders, false prophets who use the name of God to grow rich and to expand their political and economic power, live in luxury. Those leaders were acquiring mansions, imported cars and becoming more powerful at the expense of others. They were opening new temples in strategic places with large population density, such as new branches of the company that could be called "industry and market of the universal faith".

That is what really takes place in this cult: they clandestinely manufacture and market, sometimes auctioning, from stickers and key rings to discs, tapes, newspapers and books, all of this in the temples of God and in the name of the Lord Jesus. Certainly if the Lord returned today, He would enter those temples with the whip in his hand, as it is written:

"And found in the temple those that sold oxen and sheep and doves, and the changers of money sitting:

And when he had made a scourge of small cords, he drove them all out of the temple, and the sheep, and the oxen; and poured out the changers' money, and overthrew the tables;

And said unto them that sold doves, Take these things hence; make not my Father's house a house of merchandise. (John 2:14-16)"

When Grigore filed his petition, the judge could opt to not open the proceedings. In the juridical jargon that is called "initial ineptitude", i.e. the request is not convincing enough to go ahead with the proceedings. This ensures that a citizen is not suing someone simply on a whim.

When the unorthodox petition against the Universal Church fell upon his table, the judge in fact took a long time before subpoenaing the church. But in that case the reason was not the ineptitude, but the non-compliance with the paradigms of a petition. The judge would later tell Grigore that his petition "seemed a novel". And he had to read and reread it for a few days, trying to adjust not only to the out of standard language, but also to the argument combining reason and faith.

But God had a plan in the life of the petitioner: to lead him to know moral decay, the impudence and the insolence of the high administration of the Universal Church, with a seat in São Paulo. It is as if He wanted to show and to speak to him:

- My son, you gave everything you had for love to Me, to My Work. However you, as well as thousands of members of this church who really love Me, were deceived, robbed by those men, voracious wolves dressed as lambs who cynically, using My Name, took the money of the rich and of the poor, of the wealthy and, mainly, of the miserable.

Wake up my fanaticized son, your wife is right. Those men are deceitful, false prophets, who will be cast alive, without judgment, on the lake of fire burning with brimstone, as I had revealed to the apostle John, and he testified to it in Revelation (Revelation 19:20-21)

I am a God of love and compassion. I never would lead families and persons who believed in Me into misery, asking them, day after day, to give all they have.

What those cheaters are doing is to lead the people to tempt me, as My Son said when tempted in the desert by the Devil: "Thou shalt not tempt the Lord thy God." Therefore, I turned my back to them a long time ago, and the blessing and prosperity prayer they do for the people hits the ceiling and falls back, because I do not hear it, nor answer it.

In fact, it must have been a hard decision for the judge. What to do with a case in which one of the arguments was blown by God in the ear of the author? And in which any potential juridical punishment to the defendants would be added to other even worse: burn in the fire for all eternity?

Therefore the longer period of reflection was required to determine if the proceedings should be opened. In the end, Grigore's petition received the signature of Judge Carlos Ricardo Chiletto, from the 30th civil court of Rio de Janeiro, and the Universal Church of the Kingdom of God was starting to confront one of their most uncomfortable suits.

Taking Down the Mask

Grigore knew very well the way this legal bomb would explode in the Universal Church. The despair epidemics would take down the high administration, always fragile before any threat. Therefore, in the petition the former lawyer insisted on showing he was not fooling around, and the one who now was taking them to judgment had the advantage of having known them very well.

The high salary, the brand new car, the "Bishop" office had a very high price for those who fear God and practice the word of God in their lives.

The price was to obey the commander and to do things the conscience and the conduct of a true Christian would not admit. The professional ethics and the oath performed by the petitioner as an attorney prevented him from revealing them in this opportunity, however if urged and required by the competent authorities, and obtaining from the life guarantees, for fighting against a true mafia of faith, mighty and capable of everything, this petitioner hereby undertakes to reveal it, in the name of the truth, since the truth is the precise expression of what is real: it is like oil on water; always in distinction and, although it could be mixed for a short time period, sooner or later it appears, as Lord Jesus himself declared: "For there is nothing covered, that shall not be revealed; and hid, that shall not be known." (Mt.10:26)

Having included in his defense the verse of Saint Matthew's Gospel, the Universal Church certainly would know Grigore would not omit the proposal made to him to bribe a judge in the name of their interests. That ended up indeed happening. The fact was brought up during the hearings. When Grigore's suit against the Universal Church became public, he disclosed to the press what happened in the office of Bishop Edir Macedo. That and other revelations of things behind the scenes cause the ethics of the Universal Church of the Kingdom of God to be once again questioned by public opinion. In November, 1990, for instance, the title of an article in the diary Jornal da Tarde gave the size of the image associated to the Universal Church: "Mass Robbery":

We are no more before isolated cases of exploration of good faith of a humbler tier of the population. The proportions taken by this abuse are alarming, making it one of the most wicked means of organized crime existing between us.

In his final conclusions, Grigore made clear what his bold arguing strategy was.

Thus, by the word of God, Mr. Macedo, through his conduct, is perfectly characterized in the condition pointed out by the petitioner of being a false prophet.

In summary, the process would have the mission to prove that God condemns the behavior of Bishop Macedo and the Universal Church, and that He is not by his side, as they want people to believe. Technically it was a civil suit for damages, but the cause was faith.

After telling his history, Grigore concluded:

It is fully characterized, Your Excellence, by the narrative of facts and proofs, the net and certain right of the petitioner, deceived in his good faith by the greed and cleverness of the leaders of the defendant who, cunningly, using the name of God and exploiting the Christian feelings, managed to cheat him, taking, through the mentioned form, movable properties and real estate, humiliating him and putting him in misery to, after that, throw him away like used toilet paper.

Finally, he showed his intention to remove the masks of the Universal Church:

> And the will of God, clarified by the Holy Spirit in the heart of the petitioner, was to submit and facing the combat, such as little David faced and won against mighty Goliath, in the name of the Lord. Not for selfishness or just a desire for justice or enrichment, but so that the truth regarding these false prophets managing the Universal Church is finally revealed.

> Thus, thousands of worshipers, followers of the Lord in this and other cults with methods and greed by the leaders are similar, and who surely love the Lord as much or even more than the petitioner, would be capable to understand the reason for the poverty in which they live, in spite of serving to the living God, owner of all gold, silver and bronze in this world.

A common routine when a person or institution is sued is to first reach the other part to try an agreement. The Universal Church did not do that. For them, Grigore had become not just an opponent, but an enemy to be destroyed.

Answers and Rejoinders

Right in their opening, the defense made by the Universal Church showed that the target would first be the author of the accusation, and only then there would be arguments.

> The first part is really difficult to defend, not because there are facts and strong legal bases, but because it reflects a whine of the petitioner even towards himself.

> Even so, regarding the claim in judgment we must consider that in spite of the many biblical quotes and saying that he was given revelations, the facts and acts attributed by the petitioner to the defendant are not true.

This motto, that petitioner Grigore would be a problematic subject, declaring heavenly revelations and that his request is a "rosary of lamentations" would be the basis of the Universal Church's defense. The defense did not care about the faith and the divine word mentioned in the petition. Its battle would be here on earth, and the only spirit they were willing to judge would be the problematic spirit of Grigore.

In fact, in the rosary of lamentations that is the initial petition, the petitioner complains about his own improvidence, immaturity and fanaticism.

The petitioner in several passages of the initial petition says he got fanatical, he did not act with rationality, and he wishes to blame the defendant for his alleged poverty status.

The lamentation of the petitioner is so big and unreasonable that he tries to blame the defendant for his own engagement.

The petitioner laments his own lack of control and he wants to hold the defendant liable, which is inadmissible. If he, as he alleges, was selling food on credit in a business he had recently started, it is obvious that he was an awful businessman to say the least.

The petitioner shows himself as a great victim, but his character and his actions show precisely the opposite.

About the final duel of Grigore with Bishop Macedo, the strategy of the Universal Church made it clear it didn't care for things from above. For them, it didn't matter despite whether the Bishop was or not coherent with his preaching, if he was a man of God or not. The discussion that caused the termination of the former lawyer from the Universal Church was due to factors more mundane. There was no regard for the spirit, but just for matter; no discussion of faith, but of the labor relationship.

The petitioner declares he started to direct the legal department of the defendant, bought a car, had the rent paid by the church, and then "woke up" through "revelation", having thus "reprimanded" Bishop Macedo, the higher spiritual leader of the entity, being thus dismissed, what everyone must agree is perfectly normal in such situations, i.e. when the employee starts to reprimand the boss.

In other words, for the Universal Church, Grigore should take responsibility for his acts. The idea of coercion or any kind of brainwashing was promptly rejected. The task of Grigore would concern a central issue in cases like the Universal Church and similar cults: if the members are in full control of their will or if there are methods to subtract the full control of them. This was a controversial and mighty legal subject, in which the current suing might come to serve as jurisprudence for similar situations.

Aside from the primordial goal of disqualifying the source, the following argument of the Universal Church – represented by the lawyer Norton Linhares Lavoratti – was denying that all the donations exposed by Grigore had been done. I.e. the process was based on a great lie.

> Without proof of any alleged delivery or the sale of goods to the defendant, which did not happen, being that the deeds and copies of the property registers attached by the petitioner were only proof that over time performed several real estate business transactions, but there was nothing regarding these facts alleged in the initial petition.

As a guarantee, one of the defense points, however, argued preventively: even if the donations had taken place, Grigore donated because he wanted too. For that, the lawyer uses the words of Grigore himself, out of context.

> Even if the petitioner had donated goods to the defendant, the petitioner in no moment of his extensive narrative says he was forced to donate. I.e. he would have donated by free will, after biblical quotations made by the pastors 'who piously believe in what they preach to their worshipers', which already refutes any pretension to accuse the defendant pastors of bad faith while asking donations.

Only two points were reserved for the defense of the Universal Church's activities and image. In one of them, together with testimonies of worshipers in support of the church – "informed and educated persons" – the defense lawyer repeats the marketing the Universal Church usually discloses in its services: that their worshipers became prosperous after finding them.

> It is not true that the pastors providing services to the defendant have induced or induce persons to have a material detachment for the benefit of the pastor. And this is so true that it is very common to see pastor during services carried out in the Universal Churches of the Kingdom of God's preaching on the financial wealth arising from hard and persistent work in any activity.

The was another item as part of their traditional defense of the Universal Church, concerning the recovery of a "huge number of misfits" who enter their doors, added to a weird reasoning that if the Universal Church is growing, it is because it is good.

> It is not true that the defendant is a market. It has been rehabilitating many people in society from drug addicts, prostitutes and a huge numbers of social outcasts, to the point that in Rio de Janeiro the defendant was declared a public utility. This entity declared by the municipal law number 1407, from June 8th, 1989, being today. According to the BBC London, they are the church that grows faster in the world. Well, it is known that a bad plant does not grow well. So...

As expected, the Universal Church alleged that the final point in the relations between Grigore and the church was the labor agreement executed months before.

> The petitioner has no right of doing any kind of claim regarding the defendant, because, in addition to the facts narrated by him being not true, as demonstrated, on April 6th, 1992, the petitioner signed an agreement with the defendant, having received in the judgment Cr$ 23,053,704.00, corresponding to all his rights, settling them and declaring there would be nothing more to contest, "whether in labor law or civil law", being thus not allowed and indemnity claim by the petitioner against the defendant.

Grigore's counterattack was looking to undermine the Universal Church's answer point by point. He started with the most sensitive one, and the most important to the suit: the vehement denial that in the Universal Church pastors do not preach detachment in benefit of their own material attachment, and that, if worshipers donate, it is by their own free will.

That was the behavior, which ceased to be only "public and well-known", according to Grigore, and now was getting the Universal Church in the dock. The donations were a scandal whose importance the church's lawyer was candidly trying to reduce.

Therefore Grigore went deeper in exposing the tragedies unfolding during the services of the Universal Church of the Kingdom of God.

In this cult the members are asked to, in the name of Lord Jesus, donate houses, land, cars, phones, jewelry and money, inducing the people with lies and promises to not only detach from their goods, but even, before the despair of not being able to carry out the "votes with God", commit suicide. This was the recent case announced by the press and occurred with a member of the Universal Church of the Kingdom of God, in the city of Belo Horizonte.

Is it the God of love, understanding and kindness who takes whole families to misery, despair and even suicide? It certainly isn't.

The text continues bombarding the abyss that separates the life of the worshipers and that of the leaders. And it exposes the contradiction Grigore lived in the Universal Church but for so long refused to see.

Is the Lord Jesus the one who establishes or wants the false prophet Edir Macedo with money, collected by lies, from the housemaid, the unemployed father, the wealthy and the miserable, to buy an apartment assessed at more than $ 1 million in one of the most sophisticated and valued closed condominiums in São Paulo? This would be a mansion in the United States, a BMW imported car or a television broadcasting station?

This is the millionaire pastor who preaches detachment. The honorable speaker involved in illicit acts. The man who says he cures by faith but who resorts to medicine when his own health is at risk. Grigore did not save ungraceful adjectives to paint a portrait of the false prophet.

Edir Macedo, involved in inquiries arising from accusations by the Federal Police, was prosecuted for managing the Universal Church of the Kingdom of God as a clandestine financial institution, evading taxes, with a preventive arrest warrant issued and, however, a coward consumed by fear of the gift of the Holy Spirit, that for long had left him, a fugitive in the United States and submitting, through lawyers, medical evidence of illness.

The man full of the "power of God", which "cures patients", submitting medical documentation because he is sick in the United States!

That is the shame and humiliation to which is taken a man whose mind is currently possessed by a deceitful spirit, that of the devil himself, and that put him in prison and in the shameful situation he now is in.

The part stating that Bishop Macedo was abandoned by the Holy Spirit deserves a comment. Grigore thinks Macedo was one day a sincere man in his intentions. He shared this opinion, for instance, with a pastor named Roberto, of Church Nova Vida, who was beside Macedo when the Universal Church was only a group of God-fearing persons who met to pray and share their faith. It was during these times when the temples were inside the garage of a house of one of them or small sheds lent by a member who had a business. With the explosion of members – and consequently of the income – Bishop Macedo would have started to light candles for other causes. "His God now was greed, power and money", says Grigore. Now, as he says in the rejoinder, "it is precisely this filthy spirit that uses Edir Macedo to deceive and to lead thousands of people into misery".

While he was attacking and focusing his energies on the behavior of Bishop Macedo – who represented a sort of nucleus of the contradictions and deceits of the Universal Church – he also needed to defend himself. The church's attorney had used the *ad hominem* tactics, disqualifying the person in his attempt to impact the arguments. For that, some shots were aimed at Grigore as a businessman. Now he should evade the bullets and return them to their origin point, with the argument that the worst business in his life was to join the Universal Church.

The brainwashing and the fanaticism to which he was taken by the defendant in fact turned the author into an awful businessman. First for believing, according to the spiritual view of the false prophet, that God wanted to make a liberal professional, with a post-graduate education in Law and civil process, into a seller of lunch. Now, Your Excellence, as one could explain, aside by a spurious and criminal brainwashing procedure, performed by representatives of the defendant, that the same "awful businessman" before joining the cult that uses and disgraces the name of the Lord Jesus, with the practice of diabolical acts, had got, through work and strenuous negotiations, all the goods listed under item 2 of the initial petition?

The art of discussion generally uses a strategy developed by the old Greek philosopher Aristotle known as rhetoric (eristic). Centuries later, another philosopher, Arthur Schopenhauer, would define the use of eristics in the title of one of his books: How to being right. In the work, Schopenhauer compiled sophistical methods praised by a long tradition in rhetoric, in which the truth does not matter, but to win the argument. Perhaps the most classic of those strategies are to take the ideas of the adversary out of context. The Universal Church's lawyer tried to do this, attributing to Grigore the idea that pastors "piously believe in what they preach to the worshipers." Therewith Grigore had to re-contextualize the sentence, clearly defining the distinction between two social classes within the Universal Church: the commanded and the leaders. In his initial petition Grigore in fact had defended that the commanded believe in what they do. They believe in it so much they blindly follow the orders of the leaders. And the suit was targeting the latter.

It was necessary also to separate the chaff from the wheat regarding the social function of the Universal Church.

Who has been rehabilitating persons for social life, Your Excellence, is not the Universal Church of the Kingdom of God, whose leaders are examples for nobody. Those who have been rehabilitating and who always will make addicts, prostitutes and misfits a different person, new creatures, is the seed of faith introduced by the word of God in the dry hearts and then watered by the biblical teachings finds fertile land, growing and yielding good fruits, seen by any one, through the changes in behavior and in the character of the human being.

In other words: faith is a thing, the Universal Church is another thing. But what kind of thing? A thing of commerce, as Grigore first alleged and had been questioned by the answer? Grigore now agreed with the opponent.

The allegation that the defendant is not commerce is the truth. Commerce is a legalized activity creating jobs, generating income and paying taxes.

The defendant is in the segment of transactions and sales constitutes an illegal, clandestine activity, since it negotiates, within its temples, from key ring, stickers and T-shirts, to newspapers, books, discs and tapes, with no bill of sales, paying no tax and creating no jobs, since for the marketing only the little bag is used with, in addition to the pastors, workers who earn nothing to perform this activity.

For the empirical demonstration that the Universal Church was concerned less with spiritual matters and more with material matters, Grigore once again used as a weapon the arguments of the opponent. If the lawyer of the church himself was treating the relationship between Bishop Macedo and Grigore as employee and boss, and not as a spiritual leader and a worshiper, who could deny that the Universal Church was more of a company than a church?

That was in fact the sin committed by the author: to believe, after being deceived like thousands of other people in this cult, it was the work of God, performed in accordance with the teachings and commandments of the Lord Jesus and, consequently, to have bravely reprimanded Mr. Edir Macedo for the practice of acts opposed to the word of God.

In truth, currently the petitioner knows that the sign saying the Universal Church of the Kingdom of God represents only the front of a Lord's house literally hiding a large company, financial institution and commercially clandestine operation, managed by the "boss" and false prophet Edir Macedo.

Finally, Grigore responded to doctor Norton Linhares about the settlement he signed months before. It was far from being the end of that history.

Once again we need to highlight, as it was many times repeated, that the author, before a total lack of resources resulting from the severance and non-payment of his rights, was literally coerced and forced to sign, in the office of a lawyer in São Paulo, the fictitious "settlement" which also included an astonishing waiver of his civil rights, which evidently had no juridical value, due to not only the coercion circumstances under which the settlement was signed, but especially because in this petition the author is claiming as a former member of the cult, and not a lawyer or form employee.

It was the worshiper complaining, not the lawyer. The fight would go far.

From Impotent to Omnipotent

During the months following his exit from the Universal Church and while the suit was ongoing, Grigore and Nadege kept looking at a Pentecostal church in which they felt sheltered, even after the material and spiritual damage caused by the Universal Church of the Kingdom of God. Grigore explains that they learned to differentiate the faith, the praise and the true word of God from the word of men. In the case of the men of the Universal Church, their words were of little value. Therefore, it was not faith that they were looking for in other churches, but they were going there for a much more prosaic reason: to fraternize, to meet other people who praised the Holy Spirit. In summary, a place in which there was honesty in the communion with God.

The problem is they never found that place. In all other Pentecostal church's they attended —they saw the same old vices in a slightly different skin. But at least they were vaccinated. Grigore never again donated anything to the churches, even if in some of them he received from the pastors the designation of "goat kid", a nickname used to lessen and distinguish him from the "sheep", those worshipers compromised in their heart and soul.

In Church Nova Vida, to where they went after leaving the Universal Church, it didn't take long to see the contradictions again. On the pulpit, pastors who were not practicing what they were preaching. Church Nova Vida looked to the eyes of the couple more protected from the decayed environment they found in the Universal Church. It was more traditional – it was from there that the men came who later founded the Universal Church, such as Bishop Macedo and missionary R. R. Soares. Maybe the rotten apples had left because they did not manage to pollute the environment. Additionally, in New Life the audience was usually more critical and vigilant. If the Universal Church was composed of his majority by people of classes C and D, the church at Nova Vida University was comprised of students and wealthier people. These temples were more comfortable and all of them had air conditioning.

One day Grigore commented in high-spirits with the pastor – after a service in which, as in the Universal Church, someone preached against medicines, since God alone could heal – that he was not taking any medicine for his breathing problems, believing in the spiritual cure. In the back rooms, the pastor was much more prudent than in front of the audience. He said one pill or another from time to time does not hurt anyone, and even he was taking his Lexotan to relieve anxiety.

In another episode involving cures, Grigore followed a worshiper, with whom he had become friends, to speak with Bishop Walter McAlister, one of the leaders of Nova Vida. Dalmo de Paula, the friend, was suffering from a swelling with stains on his leg that no doctor could heal. It could only be a spiritual issue, they concluded. So it was nothing better than to see the spiritual leader of the church. After a long wait for Bishop Walter, the man from whom they were waiting for an inspired answer – or at least a wise word – he appeared, and went through without paying much attention to the two worshipers waiting for him on a wooden bench. Grigore and Dalmo, a little confused, followed the Bishop through the corridors of Nova Vida quickly explaining the issue, since the Bishop seemed hurried and unwilling to talk. Finally, before the decisive question – what does this man have in the leg? – Bishop Walter answered crystal clearly and impatiently: "I have no idea! I'm not God!"

It might have been only a demonstration of humbleness or mindlessness. Anyway the answer did not match the McAlister on the pulpit, introducing himself as the savior.

This was not what led Grigore and Nadege to quickly leave Nova Vida. The church ended up bringing them a familiar bad taste. A girl named Flavia, daughter of Bishop Rubens, was approaching 30 years of age and her main mission at the church was not to find God, but to find a boyfriend. One day she came to the temple and noticed the presence of a new member in charge of opening the door for the worshipers. This was the first son of Grigore, then 21 years old, who looked like the ideal prey. Flavia started to attend the church's youth group and soon they started to date. In the beginning Grigore and Nadege just found it weird that this, girl who was dating their son, didn't even greet them. Her maternal and paternal feelings soon turned into concerns. When Nadege underwent a colectomy surgery, the girl did not visit her and the only phone call she made was at 1 a.m., waking the convalescent mother to talk with her boyfriend Gregório. To her boyfriend, she used to tell that when they got married her father, leader of the church in Nova Iguaçu, would give them everything, but that Gregório could not share under no circumstances the money with his parents. The insidious presence was dividing the family, and when Gregório's parents decided to try to open his eyes, they started to hear in one of the services the sermon of Bishop Rubens, who was accusing people in the audience of boycotting the will of God and the happiness of his own daughter.

After a year and seven months, Gregório gave up on the marriage. Soon after, Flavia was engaged to a young man who she always mocked for being fat. Rogério, the new chosen one in her life, ended up fighting his whole family, and when his father, weakened in a wheelchair, tried to talk with Bishop Rubens, he was not well received. Flavia and Rogério got married after the death of Rogério's father.

This last part Grigore and Nadege followed from a distance. In fact, it only increased their disappointment with the Church Nova Vida, causing them to leave. Their children decided to keep attending the church, since they felt they were fitting in. Then one day they were expelled in the middle of a service, paying for the quarrels of their parents with Nova Vida.

They got out from one church where the pastor declared himself impotent to heal the worshipers and felt into the opposite extreme. Grigore and Nadege heard from acquaintances that there was a different, more modest church, where they didn't ask for money. During the first service they attended at the Church Maranata, they saw that the modesty was only in the number of worshipers and in the facilities. The pastor soon revealed his omnipotence. After a few moments of silence and a sort of spiritual trance the pastor cried out: "Verily, verily, I say unto you." He had received the spirit of nobody less than God. And before the incredulous look of Grigore, he confirmed with a hoarse voice, supposedly to show wisdom. "It is me in fact, the All Mighty; I came here to speak to you." Since it was carnival time, in the sermon that day the pastor-god compared the party to a seductive serpent. Grigore and Nadege did not stay to hear the end.

The next stop was Grace Church International, owned by the famous pastor and TV host R. R. Soares, who had a disagreement with Bishop Macedo in the command of the Universal Church and had founded his own church. Once again, the involvement of Grigore and Nadege lasted only one service. After an emotional speech to ask for donations including checks, Soares put the worshipers in a spiritual chain, all of them holding hands and praying. Meanwhile, he acknowledged the donations and bent casually on the pulpit. Soares broke the chain a few times to warn the worshipers. He shouted the name of one of them and then informed them: "You forgot to endorse the check."

That crossed the line and the increasingly shorter patience of Grigore. He broke the chain, freeing his hands, and left Grace Church International, giving no explanation to anyone. Soares noticed this move and did not let it go. From the pulpit, he began to curse the couple, declaring to know all the time that there was a traitor amongst them. This traitor dared to file suit against a church, and against God, he concluded.

In the last stage of their pilgrimage, a friend said she would introduce Grigore to a pastor who had played on her favorite soccer team, Botafogo. The name of the new man of faith was suggestive: Moses. The couple prepared a good dinner to receive him. When the pastor arrived, Grigore did not recognize the black and agile half-camper who he was waiting to find. The pastor was white, and in truth had played on São Cristóvão's team. After that, he tried his luck in Portugal, and was left without a team, went hungry and then had a divine revelation. A fire ball quickly entered his window, as if it came from a devastating kick, and the image of Christ appeared saying that Moses was the one chosen to carry out His work.

After that day, the player never went hungry again. Even out on the field and without money, everything he had to do was to ask his wife what she would like to eat. If the answer was chicken, ten minutes later a chicken, ready to eat appeared at their doorstep. If they wanted breakfast, they prayed and within an instant, the breakfast appeared at the door. Moses and her even tried a surprise to see the angel who was assisting them. After praying for spaghetti, they looked through the window to see if someone was entering the building where they lived. There was no movement, but the spaghetti somehow appeared.

With such obvious signs, Moses told Grigore and Nadege that together with other soccer players, such as the star Sérgio Manoel, they founded a church: Alfa-Omega, which means the beginning and the end. They invited the couple to become worshipers. The answer was no. The couple had already spent too much money to offer a dinner for that mad man, who wasn't polite enough to bring a dish from their angel delivery service.

The Bible against the Civil Code

The legal process lasted 5 years. Right after Grigore's retort, the answer of the Universal Church, now represented by Doctor Claudemir Mendonça de Andrade, was going to build a web that would take many years to undue. There was not, according to the argument of the defense "no sign" of the donations

Grigore claimed. And, preventively, if they existed they were made by the "free will" of the author.

The counterattack of the Universal Church was also demonstrating that they were not going to accept any further insolence in silence. The reiterated request to the judge was to remove "insulting expressions", and for that, they indicated that such expressions widely violated Brazilian Civil Adjective Law.

In fact, it is not likely such adjectives chosen by Grigore to designate the Universal Church and its leader are included in the Adjective Law. In his texts, Bishop Macedo had already been called a scoundrel and rascal, in addition to the commas always accompanying the term Bishop to disqualify the title, in any given moment, Macedo is reduced to "little Bishop".

"Decay", "quagmire", "soldier of the commander", "dictator" and "cheater" were only a few of the nouns Grigore used against the Universal Church and Bishop Macedo. Therefore, the defendant's lawyer decided to try to put an end to the mess, asking that those were "removed from the minutes".

Even though this action was secondary to the suit, the focus of the Universal Church's defense was already quite clear. The "insulting expressions" heard before the "great and celebrated jurist Pontes de Miranda" supported the request. Pontes de Miranda says:

The removal shall be complete and effective, i.e. in full and
not leaving any part of the offensive sentence or sentences.

Fighting against this opposition, Grigore wanted to add to the discussion, against this debate, using hard and emotional words, that the Universal Church preferred the cold, rational arguments in the technical and distant language of the Civil Code and of their commentators.

There was a reason for this tactic. In this field they knew they would still give much work to Grigore. The questions were many.

Compensation for what? From what he allegedly donated to the defendant? When, how and where is the proof? Still regarding the compensation for material and moral damages, why, or due to what? From being a member of the church?

As for the donations, the lawyer stated, "There was no sign" of them, and it was not by chance that the defense was taking this stance. After they started to reject donations of goods, the hard cash – even a large amount resulting from the sale, for instance, of an apartment –which was put in the Universal Church's little bag. I.e. between the sale and the donation the Universal Church's attorney was right: there was no sign. The little bag didn't have receipts, had no accounting, didn't even distinguish which member had donated.

The proofs regarding this fact, attached by Grigore to the proceedings, were of the purchase and sales agreements for all real estate transactions he had and were given away in favor of the church. The defense now wanted proof that Grigore got this money, went to the temple and deposited it in the little bag. An ungrateful mission considering how the things were done. For that, it was necessary to reveal this system quite comfortable for Universal Church, in which the financial connection with the worshipers was obvious, but invisible to the eyes of the law.

The burden of proof, or *onus probandi*, as used by doctor Mendonça, would not stop there. "Unquestionably, we repeat, the author presented no proof of the causal connection concerning the defendant's sermon, and his (alleged) equity loss".

That connection would be a long controversy. How to establish a cause and effect relation between a service where the audience was in an emotional state, where the pastor, a brilliant speaker, has on his side the credit of representing the divine word, and having as a result that same word leading people to empty their pockets for love – or fear – to God? How do you prove a brainwashing process that is not even provided in the Civil Code?

The process placed at the center of the court hearings was the behavior of the Universal Church of the Kingdom of God. The defense painted a picture in which its client was preaching its faith, and the behavior of the worshipers was their responsibility. Donations are a freewill offering made by those who believe and want to do it. Between the pastor on the pulpit and the crowd in the audience, there is no such causal connection for damage due to bad faith. The implicit logic is: If the pastor speaks and the member believes, who will be against us?

From the side of the accuser the case went beyond a personal matter. It was questioning the behavior of the Universal Church that bothered a majority of the public. The case was to make the Pastor and especially the leaders accountable and responsible for their actions. What the defense described as the normal church services were not what actually occurred. Between the pulpit and the audience there was a cause and effect relation, and it was scandalous.

The following – and huge – step would be to prove this cause and effect relation. The good news for Grigore is that the judge allowed his adjectives to stay in the minutes.

Suffering as a Method

It was necessary to neutralize the innocence with which the Universal Church described the donations in its temples. If brainwashing was not provided for under the Civil Code, coercion was. The Brazilian Law is not blind to religious charlatanism. Proof of this is that there is a Police Station, Specialized Against the Public Faith. It was the word of such institution, in the report from the chief officer Laércio de Carvalho, made on his visits to the Universal Church in 1989 that Grigore attached to the proceedings.

> We assiduously attended the said church for consecutive years, and what we saw there is a police case. There are five sessions a day, and in all of them millions are received in donations which they practically demanded, in money, land, small farms, cars, jewels and especially golden wedding rings.

Testimonies gathered by the Police Station were submitted. A person's destiny in Universal Church was quite different from the glorious histories seen during the services, on television and in the testimonies, the defendant's attorney had attached to the proceedings.

> I am a bank employee, married and the mother of two children. My husband was always a hardworking man who always provided for the family, but three months ago, he started to attend a church called the Universal Church of the Kingdom of God, on Celso Garcia Avenue.

> In the beginning, I liked this because I was always very religious, but soon I realized that he had changed his behavior, giving me no more money to take care of the house and the children, saying he had to give it to church, and that church was more important.

I started to complain about his behavior and the harm he was bringing to the children and me. He told me that the pastor indicated that the devil would come to take him away from the path of salvation, and that I also had to go to church so that they could take the devil out of my body.

I had to go with him, suffering threats and aggressions. What I saw and I still see in there makes it hard to believe there is in this country a pastor forces people to give all their money in exchange for miracles, deceiving the people, selling holy water, blessed oil and holy bonfire, and pressing the people to give to church all their earnings and properties.

If you went there one time you would see with your own eyes how the people are deceived and robbed, being forced to give to the pastors everything they have. They are threatened that if they are saving money to pay a bill or obligation, God will punish them, and they will have their life ruined because they are hiding that from God.

The tone in other testimony was angrier.

The last achievement of "Bishop Macedo's" boys was to ask the person (or fools?) to give the money that they saved for their water, light, or phone bill. Finally, that last savings kept only for emergencies. They assured them that on the following day a miracle would happen and the money would be returned multiplied by three."

"I was revolted when I heard the pastor asking for the bus fare from those that had nothing else to give. He said God help them find their way home together.

A social worker specialized in the Juvenile Court of São Paulo celebrated that something was being done.

In my daily work I've been watching with sorrow to an increasingly larger crowd of humble people, damaged in their scanty savings and even in their mental and psychological health by those 20th century temple vendors."

"As the person of faith that I am, I'm very glad to know that something will be done against those people thirsty for prestige and money, who do not hesitate in exploiting the pain and the faith of humble persons, using their pain for their own interests and transforming faith into the superstition and fear.

Finally, Grigore looked to demonstrate that the suffering he underwent was "standard practice of the doctors of faith". In his thesis, there was coercion, and to prove that he tried to bring to light the abyss separating the word preached to the service practices. The Universal Church defended the prosperity of the worshipers while asking them to give up their bus fare. It defended solid affective ties but only until one of the spouses turned against the church, and then he or she now was an instrument of the devil.

For the worshiper Grigore, the cause was even bigger. What was going on there was "precisely what the Lord had already foreseen two thousand years before, warning in the Scriptures". While the process advanced, Grigore was seeking each time more support in the Bible. The spiritual dimension was finally entering into the court proceedings, since the petitioner's thesis indicated that everything that was occurring prophesied by Saint Peter in the Scriptures.

But there were false prophets also among the people, even as there shall be false teachers among you, who privately shall bring in damnable heresies, even denying the Lord that bought them, and bring upon themselves swift destruction.

And many shall follow their pernicious ways; by reason of whom the way of truth shall be evil spoken of.

And through covetousness shall they with feigned words make merchandise of you: whose judgment now of a long time lingereth not, and their damnation slumbereth not.

Having eyes full of adultery, and that cannot cease from sin; beguiling unstable souls: an heart they have exercised with covetous practices; cursed children;

These are wells without water, clouds that are carried with a tempest; to whom the mist of darkness is reserved forever.

While they promise them liberty, they themselves are the servants of corruption.

Instead of quotations from juridical libraries, it was from the Bible. Grigore was making it clearer that he was not only talking about the earthly court, but also to the court of the heavens. And he would not mind at all to combine them in the process, arguing with reason and with faith. The justice of the verdict, he said, it would be doubled.

The author is aware he represents only a mere instrument lifted and calloused in the struggle, in the pain and in the humiliation he has been going through in the name of the Lord Jesus – praised and glorified be Him for all eternity – and that the ending of this process, summarized through the sentence Your Excellency will utter certainly represents a biblical landmark, i.e. a starting point from which the glass of the wrath and fury of God shall be poured.

War of Experts

The way to establish the material connection the defense was requiring as the burden of proof from Grigore – between the sale of his goods and the effective donation to church – would be through the letter of law. Decree 1.041, from January 11th 1994, establishes that charity organizations and foundations, including religious entities, were required to keep a bookkeeping of their income and expenses. It was a question then to ask the judge to check the financial books of the temples of Recreio dos Bandeirantes and Barra da Tijuca while Grigore attended there. The amount of the donations performed would be registered. The cash books would serve as a proof that everything he had had been written down in them.

The inspection went to the churches. They replied that they used accounting, but had no control of what each church received. That because, as assured by pastor José Eduardo Alves, in Recreio dos Bandeirantes, and administrator Mauro Macedo, in Barra da Tijuca, at the end of three daily services no one checked the contents received in the little bags. They were sent to the head office at the Church of Abolição. There everything was accounted for and deposited together in the bank.

Grigore questioned that. In spite of the attempt by the Universal Church to establish the impossibility of saying what money comes from who, the persons in charge admitted that the accounting from 1989 to 1991 was centralized in São Paulo. In 35 accounting book volumes that would be the object of the litigation from there on.

The volumes increased to 52 when lawyer, economist and judicial expert Antonio Maksoud was in the Universal Church's office in São Paulo. It was time to check if the donations from Barra da Tijuca and Recreio dos Bandeirantes were written off while Grigore attended there, as well as the values of the donations.

The first counterpoint appeared quickly. In accordance to Maksoud, "in the accounting of income from tithes and donations, classified as in own account, per church, were registered". He also highlighted that the "accounting has good technique, is modern, computerized, with encoded plans, with numbered accounts".

The numbers showed a correlation between the real estate and shares sold by Grigore and the revenues received. At the temple of Recreio dos Bandeirantes, since November 1989, with the participation of the new and wealthy sheep, the little bags started to become fuller. If in February that year the pastors had to be satisfied with a monthly donation of 52.30 cruzados – the new currency circulating at that time – and during the whole year rarely surpassed the ceiling of Cz$ 200.00, at the end of the year the fair weather arrived. The Christmas of the Universal Church was fatter with donations of Cz$ 1,489.30 and Cz$ 2,000.00 in November and December. In March 1990, the church of Recreio dos Bandeirantes would exceed the mark of Cz$ 6,000.00 for monthly donations, in a geometrical progression growth that would achieve Cz$ 17,756.00 by October 1990.

For the year of 1991, donations achieved an even higher level. The Cz$ 13,976.00 in January would be high compared to the cash flow of the church before Grigore, but would be nothing compared to the Cz$ 180,200.00 in April and the Cz$ 572,000.00 in November. It seemed to be at its peak, but this was only half of it. In December 1991, the temple of Recreio dos Bandeirantes received in its little bags the unbelievable sum of Cz$ 2,346,696.00. Of course, that was a time during which inflation used to increase donations, but even considering that, the rise in status of the temple was substantial. In addition, that without changing the profile of its audience, which was still comprised of humble people, but now with Grigore amongst them.

The temple of Barra da Tijuca was already born with greater luck. It was bigger and included more wealthy worshipers. In the month of his inauguration, in August 1990, already with Grigore attending the services, the donations reached Cz$ 45,519.00. Soon it jumped to Cz$ 97,797.00 and Cz$ 135,049.00 in October and November. In the following year, after a weak January of only Cz$ 73,246.98, Barra da Tijuca reached Cz$ 230,090.00 in February. It stayed between Cz$ 150,000 and Cz$ 200,000 from March to May and exploded in June, collecting Cz$ 1,373,725. It would then drop to an average of around Cz$ 200 thousand the following months and, by the end of the year, the safes were fattening again. In November 1991 the temple of Barra da Tijuca collected almost Cz$ 1.5 million and in December more than Cz$ 1.6 million.

The conclusion of this inspection was an attempt by the Universal Church to sweep their accounting of funds under the rug. The statement that there was no discrimination of the donations per church was unquestionably taken down by an outstanding accounting organization. Secondly, and most important, the money was there.

This evidence however meant nothing to the defense. In challenging the report, the Universal Church's attorney Claudemir de Andrade looked for details and more details that could be determined to be suspicious as the result of the inspection, having the effect of delaying the process. This included questioning the expert if he had ever in fact actually entered the Universal Church's office.

To contest the expert, the defense used another expert, economist and engineer Paulo Moreira Alves de Brito in the role of technical assistant. In his report he confirmed he was next to Antonio Maksoud during the whole procedure, but he complained that an independent audit was required – provided for by the courts but not compulsory – in order to prepare the conclusions. Brito also stated that the information indicated that there was no individual accounting per temple regarding the present, but not to the past. Therefore, he concludes, there had been no intention to obstruct justice.

It was enough to make the defense try to annul the whole inspection. In his answers, Maksoud admitted he in fact did not carry out in person the inspection at São Paulo. Alleging an illness, he sent an assistant. As for tax revenue per the churches, he insisted: according to Mauro Macedo and Pastor José Eduardo there was not, in the past or in any given time, individualized records.

Finally, after the battle of the experts where each detail was used to change the course of the proceedings, the data was presented. The Universal Church kept on questioning the donations. Grigore kept arguing that he was deceived in his good faith. A game comprised of objective and subjective cards was on the table. Now the judge would have to decide.

The Sentence

Before uttering his decision, Judge João Baptista Chagas Filho asked the underlying critical question of the history of Grigore with the Universal Church of the Kingdom of God: "Can fanaticisms induce someone to the full alienation of his goods?"

His sentence may be read as an attempt to look for an answer to this delicate question, which exceeded even the relationship between the petitioner and the defendant of the suit. The bottom line was to investigate the mechanisms between worshipers and the spiritual leaders who appeared with the explosion of the so called autonomous Pentecostalism, classified as "the great current religious Brazilian phenomenon". The Universal Church was the main expression of such phenomenon.

These Pentecostal churches are greatly different from their classic parent churches, originating in the beginning of the 20th century in the American missionary movement. Now, the sentence analysis, these churches are based "in a triad: cure, exorcism, prosperity".

To understand the mechanisms involved in the relations between worshipers and pastors, the judge brought elements from social psychology, describing the need individuals have to belong to groups – especially if they are anxious individuals with emotional issues, tending to look at colleagues in the same situation.

The next step is to act in full harmony with the group, being afraid to be different and lose the emotional rewards the group brings. When someone disagrees, the judge defends; the trend is to retake "the way followed by most of the group", in a feeling called "group pride". The metaphor of the sheep having their pastor as a guide was quite relevant, considering the group behavior of sheep.

The pastor, the sentence continues, was the leader able to influence the group. This suggested that it might lead to "trance" and "purification". There caused "the deliriums, with prodigal donations and collective healings".

The psychological assessment of Grigore caused things to become more complicated. "It is necessary to notice the psychological unstable state of the author when joining a so called Christian cult; he became a baptized Jew and, at the same time, a Jewish Christian."

"Adding to that complete psychological instability there was the preaching during the services, inducing the followers to be accepted, with no opposition, the requirements of this cult." And the conclusion: "There is total domination over their will."

To exemplify, the magistrate included historical facts. The sentence mentioned "White Brotherhood", a Ukraine fanatic cult in which members were arrested for trying to destroy the very traditional Cathedral of Saint Sofia, built in the 11th century. What was the justification for their vandalism? They were preparing themselves for the Day of Judgment.

The collective suicide of the followers of the North American pastor Jim Jones was stated. On November 11, 1978, in Guyana near the border to Venezuela, the largest collective suicide known had occurred. The 914 members of the cult the Temple of the People were found dead, most from having drunk a mixture of orange juice, cyanide and painkillers. Those who refused to drink were shot by the others. Not being limited to countries abroad, the hearing also recalled the fanaticism of the followers of Antonio Conselheiro, the messianic leader who, with his group of islanders, resisted the Army until their death in the city of Canudos.

In the Universal Church, the conclusion is that fanaticism is reverted in donations. "There is then no concern at all with the donors: if they are prodigal or wasteful or if the donations embezzle their equity to the point to lead them into misery", the text says.

Chagas Filho dedicated two and a half pages of his sentence to a point that for Grigore was critical: the misinterpretation of the biblical words as a role in the Universal Church. The magistrate started from the testimony of the pastor and then assembly member Paulo Caesar de Velasco, who had defended that "the tithe is an obligation of the Christian, and the donation is a demonstration of love." And reinforced: "The word of God teaches that the more generously you are in the donation, the more reward the donor will receive from God."

The judge throws a light over this Universal Church philosophy going back to the Reformation proposed by Martin Luther in the 16th century, which opposed the authority of Church to reconstruct the written scripture. The creator of Protestantism was in the minutes, bringing the dimension of faith Grigore sought. The Bible, according to Luther, is "for itself very certain, easy, open; it is its own interpreter".

Scholars such as G. Ebeling helped the case indicating the risk of the Bible "being manipulated in its construction". The magistrate concludes: "If there is no presence of the spiritual in the literal, the text may be manipulated". To avoid that, it is necessary to observe "the context, the structure, the form, as well as the intention of the statements". On the contrary, fundamentalism would result. In addition, he concludes with the sentence:

> It is thus fundamental at the hands of the pastor and state assembly member that, in Malachi 3.10, the tithe is an obligation, since the coetaneous circumstances in which it was written were not analyzed. Other interpretations of quotations mention compulsory contribution by Christians are also fundamental.

> It is public information and well known that the fundamental reading of the texts is being, in our days, very much practiced by those new cults within the so-called autonomous Pentecostalism.

The faith and the sacred text, as Grigore indicated, were a part of the scenery. The sentence ended up being so peculiar – and significant – aligned with the petitions presented by Grigore. The Law of men might, and should, handle the questions of the spirit. The judge considered this path to utter his sentence. "It is thus correct to conclude for the psychological inducement within the defendant."

Going further, Chagas Filho decided to check for himself how the psychological induction occurred. "The judge observed in person, during several visits to such temples, that music played a fundamental role", he narrates. "Initially slow and tearful, it gradually increases, in the cadence dictated by the inflammation of the pastor, until filling everyone with euphoria, in which the pastor guides the collective purification. Hysteria is then achieved. 'Exorcisms' are performed, the pastors shouting and workers invoking the names of several

African religion entities (Maria Padilha, Zé Pelintra, Tranca Ruas etc.) saying they 'burn' them in the name of Jesus and thus they free the worshipers from those devils and from the evil they bring to the bodies of those possessed."

It is a cathartic-affective experience, and then the leaders, very charismatic and infused with God, make appeal for generous donations. The workers leave collecting the donations and distribute envelopes so that, during the next service, more donations come, in addition to the tithes.

That is the behavior to willfully induce persons of low self-esteem, taking from them, with promises of cure and prosperity, all of their goods and finances that they can.

In this last sentence it is important to highlight the term "willfully". Civil law establishes differences between willful deception and mistake. In the mistake, the responsibility belongs to the individual, who acted mistakenly due to ignorance or any other reason concerning only him. That was what the Universal Church's defense team tried to attribute to Grigore.

In willful deception, the individual is induced to the mistake. The sentence made the distinction of quoting the jurist Clovis Bevilacqua:

Willful deception is the stratagem or astute means employed to induce someone to the practice of an act that prejudices him, and benefits the author of the willful act or third party.

Judge Chagas Filho did not accept the church's charter that it only accepts donations from those who want to. "This willful deception falsifies the permission, since through fraud creates false grounds which corrupt the will".

Grigore, in the evaluation of the sentence, was one person before becoming a member of the church and another one after. Before, he was successful; after, he sold his equity in record time through bad business. The promise of peace and prosperity seduced an instable psyche. In this case, anyone "consciously taken advantage", according to the words of jurist Caio Mario da Silva Pereira quoted in the sentence, "from such inferiority a situation, even if temporary, and performing a business resulting in abnormal profit", such in fact annul any agreement, even the alleged faith agreements carried out within the Universal Church's temples.

For the judge it was therefore enough proof that Grigore had been deceived. On the truthfulness of the donations, the insistence of the defense in denying them ended up causing the church an even bigger problem. According to the Brazilian Constitution, all religious institutions are free from paying taxes. But, remember the judge, "such an exemption comprises only the equity, income and services related to the essential purposes of the entities". To have the right to the tax exemption, the Universal Church should follow its own statute, which says that "local churches shall submit monthly balances" and that the money taken should be intended for use to the "maintenance of the local services and general causes of the church".

In the process, what was seen was the statement of the leaders themselves that the Universal Church accounting was fully centralized, and they even lied saying there was no discrimination per church. The amendment went out worse that the original. "With the behavior pointed out by the inspection of the resources known as a slush fund is evidenced, as a way to evade taxes", the judge sentenced. "It is tax evasion using the gaps in the constitutional text."

Therefore, if the Universal Church was not able to register donations even per worshiper – which was an obligation to meet article 1.175 of the Civil Code, which states that, "there is null the donation of every good, without reservation of a part, or of enough income for the subsistence of the donor" – the burden of proof was now reverted. There was a correlation between the sale of Grigore's patrimony since he joined the church and the values of cash in the books: the Universal Church, which "does not have the accounting deserving credit", should now prove that it was not the same money.

In view of all of this, the suit ended challenging the behavior of the Universal Church of the Kingdom of God that until then was acting without opposition. The scandalous nature of its services was receiving an answer. Their actions of neglecting the law and not caring for a clarified sector of society, which was shocked with the things going on in the temples, got brakes in the verdict of Judge Chagas Filho. The Universal Church was sentenced to return to Grigore all real estate, shares and the car that went into their revenue, including interest and monetary correction, in addition to the equivalent of 200 days wages for moral damages.

Restarting

The Universal Church, as expected, appealed. This process added another 246 pages of documentation. In a higher court, the appeal judges reversed the sentence. By a vote of 2 to 1, the case against the Universal Church was overturned.

One single vote, however, was the most valuable, since the reporting judge cast it. In his report, the sentence in favor of Grigore was maintained, but decreasing to half the amount of the compensation. Being the reporting judge the one who knows the process better, Grigore had the right to an extra appeal, called *embargos infringentes*. Now there were five appeal judges who would consider the case presided by the chairman of the Court. This time, it was an easy win. In a vote of 4 to 1, the decision of the higher court reporting judge would be upheld.

The court would still calculate the value of the goods donated by Grigore, updating the amounts. In this case Grigore's estimate of R$ 600 thousand was confirmed and the compensation would be R$ 300 thousand. With the higher courts decision, Grigore had already the right to enter a provisional enforcement to receive a value that at the time would be fundamental.

To get a job was even harder for Grigore after his conflict with the church became public. Not only did the evangelical segment close their doors, but also Grigore was finding resistance with companies from any segment where he offered his talents as a lawyer. He started to be seen as a whistle blower, the employee who challenges the boss.

On the other hand, the Universal Church would not facilitate the enforcement of the suit. It was only then that the lawyers of the church decided to contact Grigore looking for an agreement. They were willing to pay R$ 150 thousand – i.e. half of the half of the value Grigore considered fair and agreed by the first initial sentence – but on the other and they would not appeal to the highest instance, the Upper Court of Justice, where the process could be dragged out for many years. It was a take it or leave it offer.

Without alternatives, Grigore took it. The agreement was ratified, prevailing permanently over the merit of the sentence of Judge João Baptista Chagas Filho, but with the decreased value of the compensation. Family cash was zero once again, and if the amount received was largely below what he had donated, at least the case was resolved. The family celebrated not only the influx of money but also finally a settlement with their past in which justice prevailed.

Now they had to find a direction for their lives. In the Rio de Janeiro the paths were obstructed. In 2002, five years after the proceedings, Grigore was still living on juridical temporary jobs, money income was little and the friends disappeared. The children returned to a private school and got into college. They were living in a rented apartment-hotel, where they were seen as non-rich foreigners out of their environment. They had debts to pay. The money that seemed a lot at first was fading.

Therefore, the idea of leaving Rio de Janeiro was considered in talks and prayers. One day Grigore and Nadege left their already grown children at home and simply went out travelling, with no definitive course. The sister of Nadege from Juiz de Fora was then living in the inland of the state of Sergipe. They visited them and from there the couple continued to the capital Aracaju. There they found a good apartment, easy to rent, which was very different from Rio de Janeiro, where there were several requirements, including an impossible guarantor.

During the same trip, Grigore met a former professor of Law, who spoke about job opportunities in the area. In one instance, employment and dwelling was appearing. The doors began to open, even if in Aracaju, a city known by the power of traditional families, a circle in which few manage to enter.

Gradually Grigore was conquering his place in the sun in Northeast Brazil, being particularly grateful to the people from Sergipe, who welcomed him and helped him to rescue his self-esteem and professional credibility. He was nominated and became a federal attorney. Later, professor of Civil Law at the University of Tiradentes, which had a huge campus and first line structure, including a library with 120 thousand volumes. Among the particular colleges, it is the best option, only competing with Federal University, which is public. His two sons, Gregório and Emiliano, graduated in Law from that very University of Tiradentes. They are now working and started their own families after marrying young women from Sergipe.

Grigore and Nadege live with dignity in a noble area of the city of Aracaju. Occasionally they go on vacation and travel around the surrounding privileged touristic region. In one of their last trips, in Mangue Seco, on the border with the state of Bahia – a backdrop for the soap opera Tieta – they amused themselves on the dunes with buggy rides. They were not bothered seeing pastors from the Universal Church driving in a Toyota along the beach and asking for votes for candidates of the church.

Another advantage of their new life is that nobody knows them, at least not until the publication of this book. For nine months, Grigore reflected before filing the suit against the Universal Church, and then another nine years went by until he decided to tell his history.

For that purpose, Grigore was in Rio de Janeiro, in July 2006, and asked the Judge of the 30th Civil Court, where the process was judged, to reopen it. From the sentence, a point had been left unsolved. Considering that, the sentence mentioned slush funds in the Universal Church of the Kingdom of God, as well as charlatanism and witch doctoring, requests were forwarded to the General Public Prosecution Office and to Federal Revenue Office of Rio de Janeiro, to investigate these facts. However, this was not in the minutes about any results, since 1995. Without means and availability to investigate the reason of the non-existence of answers about the foregoing requests, Grigore asked the Judge to reopen the case, reiterating and issuing new requests to investigate the illicit actions included in the sentencing. With the trade requests in hand, Grigore took them to the General Public Prosecution Office and to the Federal Revenue Office. The 28th Prosecution Office determined to immediate open a criminal inquiry, under the 44th Police Station with number 3413/2006. The civil process ended in a criminal process - n. 2006.001.165754-7. The Universal Church of the Kingdom of God is being investigated once again. One more restarting!

In its representation part, the illustrious Prosecutor of Justice Renata de Vasconcellos Araújo Bressan states:

> "Analysis of the facts, the crime of fraud is seen, with continued criminal activity, practiced by the managers of the Universal Church of the Kingdom of God, against the author of the aforementioned compensation suit, Dr. Grigore Avram Valeriu, facts occurred from 1988 to 1991, in view of illicit advantages acquired damaging others, using practices consisting of fanatical means employed against the worshipers.
>
> In theory, it is also seen the practice of the crime of money laundering, typified in art. 1 of Law n. 9.613/98, since the resources obtained with the donations performed to the Church, which showed at the time to be a true criminal organization, had as their origin,

disposition and transactions hidden and furtive, as evidenced by the inspection then performed.

It is required to mention, finally, the hypothesis of tax evasion crime. That because, even considering the tax immunity assured to temples of any religion (article 150, clause VI, paragraph "b" of Federal Constitution), including the Universal Church of the Kingdom of God, its practices showed that the essential purpose of the cult was not spiritual, but patrimonial, like a true company disguised as a temple."

In addition, the representation is finished as follows:

"Considering, however, that the maximum penalty in abstract for the crimes we listed in article 171 of CP and 1 of Law 8.137/90 is 5 years, it is necessary to acknowledge that, from the date of the facts until now, more than 12 years has passed, reason why the prescription applies (article 109, clause III of CP)."

Then, the filing of the criminal process was requested and granted.

With all due respect, the representation performed by the illustrious prosecutor is not true in a fundamental point. When reporting that, "in 1995 the judgment established *a quo* the extraction of copy of part of the judicial process and its sending to the State Public Prosecution Office and to the Federal Revenue. However, such copies were misplaced (it is not known where) and only in the current year, 2006 were such facts surfaced of the knowledge of the public prosecution, arising this police inquiry."

Grigore remembers perfectly and clearly that during the second semester of 1995 the clerk, designated to take care of the suit proposed against the Universal Church, called Paulo Leão, showed a document sent by the General Public Prosecution Office as an answer to request n. 246/95, through which the public prosecution stated that it was not under its competence to verify the facts pointed out in the aforementioned request. The signatory of this document was Dr. Hugo Jerke - Justice Prosecutor and a name known by Grigore, since he was his teacher, in 1985, at the postgraduate course of Civil law and Civil Process administered by the College Estácio de Sá, in Rio de Janeiro.

Why then did the General Public Prosecution Office initially alleged lack of competence to act, allowing those illicit acts to subsequently prescribe, in 2006, when appointed through the State Public Prosecution Office?

Only the Public Prosecution Office of the State of Rio de Janeiro has competence and presumably the obligation to answer the question above.

And how about the requests sent by the judgment to the Federal Revenue, requesting verification and reasonable measures, in view of slush funds in the accounting of Universal Church, as pointed out by the court sentence?

The subject remains without solution and with no information of any kind, in spite of several requests made in this sense, via e-mail, to the Federal Revenue Ombudsman's Office. Believe me!

To open the vault of memories, for Grigore, was not only for personal purification. He believes that to tell the truth about the Universal Church can be the beginning of "pouring the glass of the wrath of God". Initially over the false prophets who are proliferating, not only in the Universal Church, but also in other evangelical churches. Those that use similar methods, providing that there is no forgiveness for them - their destiny is the same of the devil and his demons, as written in the Revelation "Re. 19:20-21".

Concurrently, to show the truth and to unmask the deceivers means to "open the eyes" and to demonstrate the compassion and concern of God with the believers who love Him, but need to be saved and inherit eternal life, to urgently understand that following false prophets - blind guides, could lead them to their same destiny, for it is written:

"Can the blind lead the blind? Shall they not both fall into the ditch?"
(Lk. 6:39).

Grigore does not keep a grudge or resentment for the men who deluded him and humiliated him. That is in the past!

Recently, in May 2016, nine years after the book had been initially written and published, the Lord revealed the following: Grigore was only an instrument of a history that would serve as an alert to wake the conscience of Christians deceived by false prophets and, also, a permanent sign for all those practicing iniquities, independently from color, race, or religion, for the glass of the wrath of God is starting to be manifested "all ungodliness and unrighteousness of men" (Romans 1:18).

First, the following must be clarified: **the beast mentioned in the book of Revelation (Ap. 13:1) represents the Antichrist who, shortly, will be physically** revealed in the figure of a world-wide sovereign, entitled by Satan, whose power and authority will stretch out to all world, with the purpose of tormenting and persecute all those whose faith is deposited in Christ Jesus.

The great tribulation will then start, with the cups of the last plagues, similar to those sent by God in Egypt (Exodus 7:3-5), being spilled over the face of Earth, as proclaimed by the book of life "Revelation 15 and 16".

The reader may be asking the following question: at the present aren't there plagues, destruction, wars and abominable cruelty in this world?

Yes, Grigore answers, they exist, however the plagues currently poured out by God, as described in the book of Revelation (Ap. 5, 6, 8, 9 and 11), with the intention to yield the last call to repent and that, therefore, show only partial judgment.

The cups, however, identify the execution of the final judgment that will include everyone, indistinctly; at that time, there will be no more hope for repentance, as a premise of the divine pardon, since the people, regardless of the intensity of the suffering, will have lost the capability of repenting (Revelation 16:9).

The signs indicate, implacably, the nearing of the great tribulation, because the gospel is about to being fully preached unto all those that dwell on the earth (Revelation 14:6) and, as a consequence, the fury of God will be manifested over all impiety and injustice of men.

Thus, Grigore reiterates the essence of the revelation the Lord made to him, extended to all those who come to believe in this prophecy: "repent from thy iniquities and do not practice them anymore, for little, very little time remains for repentance!"

The will tell! Amen.